AQA

Self Study Guide

Isabel Alonso de Sudea

OXFORD
UNIVERSITY PRESS

Contents

Here's a reminder of the topics you have studied for AS Level and which you now need to revise.

Media

▶ Television
▶ Advertising
▶ Communication Technology

Popular Culture

▶ Cinema
▶ Music
▶ Fashion / Trends

Healthy Living / Lifestyle

▶ Sport / Exercise
▶ Health and well-being
▶ Holidays

Family / Relationships

▶ Relationships within the family
▶ Friendships
▶ Marriage / partnerships

You will be taking two examinations:

Unit 1: Listening, Reading and Writing

This paper is worth **70%** of your AS Level (and **35%** of the full A Level) and the time allowed is 2 hours.

There are three sections:

▶ Listening and Reading
▶ Reading and Writing
▶ Writing

Unit 2: Speaking Test

The Speaking Test is worth **30%** of your AS grade (and **15%** of the full A Level).
The test lasts 15 minutes and you have 20 minutes to prepare beforehand.
You are not allowed to use a dictionary.

There are two sections:

▶ Discussing a stimulus card
▶ General conversation on topics you have studied.

**Pass grades for this examination range from A down to E.
Here's an idea of what you need to be able to do:**

If you pass AS Level Spanish with an A grade, it means you can:

▶ clearly understand spoken language, including details and people's opinions.

▶ work out what someone is trying to say even if they don't spell it out in detail.

▶ clearly understand written texts, understanding both the gist and the details.

▶ talk fluently, giving your opinions and justifying them, and using a good range of vocabulary and generally accurate pronunciation.

▶ organise your ideas and write them up well in Spanish.

▶ write using a wide range of vocabulary and grammatical structures without making many mistakes.

If you pass AS Level Spanish with an E grade, it means you:

▶ show some understanding of spoken Spanish, even if you have difficulties when the language is complex and miss some of the details.

▶ can sometimes work out what someone is trying to say even if they don't give all the details.

▶ understand straightforward written texts, although you don't always understand more difficult writing.

▶ can talk in Spanish, and convey basic information, perhaps a little hesitantly and relying on material you have learned by heart. There is probably some English influence on your pronunciation.

▶ can convey information in writing, perhaps with some difficulty in organising your material and expressing it.

▶ use a range of vocabulary and structures, but quite often you make mistakes.

Preparing for the exams

You can see from these lists that when planning your revision there are really six areas you need to practise:

Speaking
Listening
Reading
Writing
Vocabulary
Grammar

There are tips on how to prepare each area overleaf.

Speaking

▶ Take every opportunity to practise speaking Spanish – in lessons, with the language assistant, with a friend, with anyone you know who speaks Spanish.

▶ Take an oral question from your textbook and work out a few sentences to answer it, then record them on tape and listen to see what areas still need practice – perhaps fluency, pronunciation or good use of vocabulary and structures.

▶ Don't write everything down first. You won't have a script on the day! You can write a few key words down for reference, but definitely no full sentences.

Listening

▶ Keep listening to Spanish, ideally every day. Use a mix of extracts you have worked on and new texts.

▶ Try listening to something for which you have the transcript. Just listen first, then listen again with the transcript and, if necessary, look up unknown words. Finally listen again without the transcript and challenge yourself to understand everything.

▶ Watching films is excellent listening practice and watching more than once is even better! Try watching with the subtitles and then without. If you find this hard going, just re-watch a short extract.

▶ Spanish radio and TV programmes are useful, but can also be difficult. Record an extract and listen or watch it more than once. You will find it gets easier.

▶ Make sure you do some exam listening practice too!

Reading

▶ Keep reading a mix of things you read once quickly, such as a magazine, and things where you work hard at a short passage and try to understand everything. Texts from your textbook are useful for this.

▶ It's useful to note new vocabulary from your reading, but don't make it such hard work that you give up. Note, say, three new words from each text.

▶ Try a 'dual-language' reading book, where you get the original Spanish on one page and an English translation on the opposite one. This is an excellent way to practise reading longer texts without losing heart!

▶ Search on the Internet for articles in Spanish on any topic which interests you.

Writing

▶ Practise planning essay questions. Jot down ideas for each paragraph – in Spanish! – along with key vocabulary.

▶ Take a key paragraph from a piece of marked work, write some English prompts to remind you of its content and then write it out from memory. Concentrate especially on sections where the teacher suggested improvements.

▶ Look carefully at marked work and identify what grammar errors you are making. Then check them in a grammar book and try some practice exercises.

▶ Make sure you are learning key vocabulary for each topic area, so that whichever subject comes up you will have some impressive words to use.

Vocabulary

▶ Learn lists of words regularly and build in time to go back over words you learned a week or two ago. Reinforcement makes them stick!

▶ Choose a system of recording new words which works for you. It could be paper lists, small sections on individual cards, recording the words and their English meanings on tape, making posters to stick on your bedroom wall ... what's important is that you are noting the words and going over them regularly!

▶ You were probably encouraged to use a good range of vocabulary in the essays you wrote during the year. Go back over them, highlighting good words and phrases and writing the English in the margin, then use this to test yourself. Words are often easier to learn in context.

Grammar

▶ Keep doing practice exercises in areas where you know you are weak.

▶ Use reading texts to practise thinking grammatically. For example, highlight a selection of adjectives, then write out the English for the phrases in which they appear. Test yourself by reproducing the Spanish phrases accurately, complete with all the correct agreements!

▶ Keep learning from your verb tables until you know all the forms of each tense of regular verbs and the most common irregular verbs. Test yourself using a die: 1 = *yo*, 2 = *tú*, 3 = *él / ella / usted*, 4 = *nosotros*, 5 = *vosotros*, 6 = *ellos / ellas / ustedes*. Use a verb list, choose an infinitive and a tense at random, throw the die and say the correct form of the verb. Practise until you can do it without hesitation.

The Speaking Test: what you need to know

The test has two parts: discussing a stimulus card and conversation on the topics you have studied.

Discussing a stimulus card (5 minutes)

Choose one of the two cards you are given and spend the preparation time on it.

▶ Prepare an answer of two to three sentences for the first question, which is usually '¿De qué trata esta tarjeta?'

▶ The other questions often ask for reasons, opinions, ideas for or against something. Think widely and come up with two or three ideas, not just one!

▶ The conversation will move onto broader issues, which will be linked to the topic. Try to imagine what else you could be asked and think what answer you would give.

▶ You are allowed to make notes. Don't write out exactly what you will say, but do note some useful vocabulary for the topic.

To do well on this section you need to have a wide range of ideas and to develop them, by giving your opinions, your own ideas, reasons and examples. Your knowledge of grammar is also important – try to use some of the vocabulary and structures you have learned during the AS course, but stick to those you feel you can use fairly accurately.

Conversation on the topics you have studied (10 minutes)

This will be on three of the four topics you have studied:

▶ Media
▶ Popular Culture
▶ Healthy Living and Lifestyle
▶ Family and Relationships

You can choose the first topic. None of the topics will overlap with the material from the stimulus card. You will be asked questions on various aspects of the topic and the examiner will pick up on the things you say and ask you to explain or develop them further. So, be careful to mention only things you are happy to discuss further!

This section is marked on four aspects:

▶ fluency, which means speaking at a reasonable speed, although you may need time to think between utterances.

▶ interaction, i.e. answering what you are asked, but also taking the lead sometimes and giving more details.

▶ pronunciation and intonation, which really means sounding as 'Spanish' as possible.

▶ grammar – see the notes above.

Television   **¿Qué tipo de telespectador eres?**

Questions

¿De qué trata esta tarjeta?

¿Cuáles de estos programas son «telebasura»?

¿Por qué son tan populares los programas «reality»?

A ti ¿te gusta ver las noticias en la televisión?

En tu opinión ¿la televisión tiene un papel positivo en la vida de hoy?

Prepare detailed answers to the questions. Look at these answers to the first question. They are all possible responses, but they get better as they get fuller and more detailed.

▶ *Trata de la televisión.*

▶ *Hay preguntas sobre varios programas de la televisión.*

▶ *Trata de los diferentes tipos de programas de la televisión. Quieren saber mi opinión sobre varios programas, por ejemplo las noticias o los reality. También preguntan acerca del papel de la televisión en nuestra vida actual.*

Family relationships   Una familia de hoy

Questions

¿De qué trata esta tarjeta?

¿Cuál es la relación entre Conchita y Miguel?

¿Será difícil para Marta llevarse bien con Jaime?

Un hermanastro, ¿de qué forma es distinto a un hermano?

En tu opinión, ¿por qué hay tantas familias con padres separados hoy en día?

The last three questions ask you to think of ideas and opinions. To answer such questions well, try to have several ideas ready; three is a good number! For example, to answer the fourth question, you could say:

Un hermanastro es distinto porque tiene un padre o una madre diferente. También ha vivido la primera parte de su vida en otra casa con otros parientes / abuelos. Tal vez tiene otras costumbres y otros amigos. Tal vez va a un colegio diferente.

Read this student's answers to the five questions from Speaking Test 2.

¿De qué trata esta tarjeta?
La tarjeta presenta a una familia imaginaria de hoy en día. El padre vive separado de la madre y de los hijos.

¿Cuál es la relación entre Conchita y Miguel?
Antes estaban casados pero ahora están divorciados y Conchita se ha casado otra vez, con Jaime.

¿Será difícil para Marta llevarse bien con Jaime?
Depende de la situación entre su madre y su padre verdadero. Creo que si se llevan bien y Marta puede ver a su padre con frecuencia entonces no estará demasiado triste. Si Marta comprende que su madre está muy contenta entonces imagino que también estará contenta.

Un hermanastro ¿de qué forma es distinto a un hermano?
Pues, es diferente porque no ha vivido en la misma familia durante la primera parte de su vida. Ha tenido una madre o padre diferente y seguramente la / lo quieren mucho todavía. Posiblemente quiere mucho a sus otros abuelos y también querá quedarse en su otra casa. Un hermano habrá sufrido el divorcio contigo y comprende mejor la situación – pero es posible que un hemanastro también pueda llegar a ser un buen amigo.

En tu opinión ¿por qué hay tantas familias con padres separados hoy en día?
Es un asunto bastante complicado de contestar porque hay muchas razones diferentes. A veces es porque los padres se casaron jóvenes sin pensar en el futuro; a veces es porque hay distintas costumbres en la familia, sobre todo si son de diferentes nacionalidades. También es posible que haya problemas de dinero o con los hijos y discutan sobre el colegio.

Now the examiner will ask other questions on the same general topic area. Here are some examples:
- ¿Qué otros problemas crees que puede haber para una familia de padres divorciados? ¿Hay algunas ventajas en tu opinión?
- ¿Qué papel tienen los abuelos en la familia de hoy en día?
- ¿Cómo imaginas que será la familia en cincuenta años?

You will be asked questions on three of the four topic areas. These pages suggest sample questions for each section. Practise answering them, then try thinking up more questions of your own for each section. That's a good way to revise the material you have covered and to try and predict what you might be asked.

Media

▶ ¿Crees que ves demasiado la tele?

▶ ¿Qué tipo de programa prefieres?

▶ ¿Qué opinas de los programas «reality»?

▶ ¿Hay suficientes programas para la gente de tercera edad?

▶ ¿Piensas que hay demasiada publicidad hoy en día?

▶ ¿Por qué no prohibir toda clase de propaganda para el alcohol y el tabaco?

▶ ¿Qué problemas habría si no hubiera más publicidad?

▶ ¿Crees que los teléfonos móviles son esenciales?

▶ ¿Piensas que Internet está lo suficientemente bien supervisado?

▶ ¿Desde qué edad se debería permitir usar Internet a los niños?

If you make a general statement, back it up with examples. For example, you are discussing celebrities and say you think that 'Las personas famosas deberían de dar un buen ejemplo a la gente'. This has more weight if you follow it up by saying 'Por ejemplo, admiro a David Beckham porque tiene proyectos para animar a los jóvenes a participar en el deporte'.

Popular Culture

▶ ¿Es verdad que solamente las películas de gran presupuesto pueden tener éxito?

▶ ¿Crees que la mayoría de los jóvenes tienen más interés en el cine que en la literatura?

▶ ¿Prefieres ir al cine o ver un DVD?

▶ Cuéntame de una buena película que has visto recientemente.

▶ ¿Qué tipo de música prefieres y porqué?

▶ ¿Cómo imaginas que será la música en el futuro?

▶ ¿Es necesario tener los mismos gustos de música que tus amigos?

▶ ¿Crees que tu ropa es parte de tu personalidad?

▶ ¿Cómo han cambiado los pasatiempos y el tiempo libre desde la juventud de tus padres?

▶ Habla un poco sobre una persona famosa que admiras.

Healthy Living / Lifestyle

- ▶ ¿Crees que los deportes tradicionales se han pasado de moda hoy en día?
- ▶ ¿Por qué se hace deporte?
- ▶ ¿Hacen suficiente deporte en tu colegio?
- ▶ ¿Cómo puedes mantener la forma si no te gusta el deporte?
- ▶ ¿Cuál presenta el mayor peligro para una persona jóven – el alcohol, el tabaco o la droga?
- ▶ ¿Qué entiendes por 'comer sano'?
- ▶ ¿Qué actividades diarias son las más peligrosas para la salud?
- ▶ ¿Qué importancia tienen las vacaciones para ti?
- ▶ ¿Hay puntos negativos acerca del turismo?
- ▶ ¿Qué otra cosa se puede hacer durante las vacaciones, además de viajar?

> Remember that the examiner will respond to what you say, so be careful to introduce ideas you are happy to talk about! Here are three possible ways to begin answering the same question: *¿Qué importancia tienen las vacaciones para ti?*
>
> - ▶ *Para mí representan una manera de evitar el estrés de todos los días. Por ejemplo, …*
> - ▶ *Lo que más me importa es pasar el tiempo con mis amigos. Me gusta sobre todo …*
> - ▶ *Me gusta ir de vacaciones a lugares donde se respeta el medio ambiente. Por eso prefiero hacer cámping y …*

Family / Relationships

- ▶ ¿Qué papel desempeñan los padres en la vida de una persona joven de 17 a 18 años?
- ▶ ¿Cuáles son los puntos de conflicto entre los jóvenes y los otros miembros de la familia?
- ▶ ¿Te gustaría más ser hijo único o tener hermanos y hermanas?
- ▶ ¿Crees que el modelo de dos padres y dos hijos es el mejor de todo?
- ▶ ¿Tus amigos son más importantes para ti que tu familia?
- ▶ ¿Te disputas con tus amigos? ¿Acerca de qué?
- ▶ ¿Cuáles son las características de un buen amigo / una buena amiga?
- ▶ ¿Crees que el matrimonio tiene importancia todavía hoy en día?
- ▶ ¿Cómo crees que es posible mitigar los efectos sobre los hijos si los padres se divorcian?
- ▶ ¿Cuáles son las ventajas de quedarse soltero/a?

> Take the lead in the discussion on occasions. If the examiner makes a point you don't agree with, don't be afraid to say so! For example, suppose you are discussing the benefits and drawbacks of being single and the examiner says 'Pues sí, tienes mucha más libertad cuando eres soltero/a'. You could respond 'Vale, pero hay también inconvenientes. Uno se puede sentirse aislado a veces y no tienes siempre alguien, por ejemplo cuando tengas un problema que quieras discutir'.

You can plan your time as you wish, but there are suggested amounts of time to spend on each section

Listening and Reading (35 marks)

Suggested time: 30 minutes

There will be about five minutes of recording altogether and you will be able to play it and pause it yourself. There will be one passage with English questions on it and two to four more passages with other types of question in Spanish, for example:

▶ reading statements and deciding which speaker said those things

▶ matching sentence halves

▶ multiple choice questions.

Reading and Writing (40 marks)

Suggested time: 45 minutes

There will be three or four passages of Spanish to read, with a variety of types of question, for example:

▶ marking statements true / false / not mentioned or positive / negative / both

▶ deciding which of a list of statements summarises a particular person's viewpoint

▶ answering questions in Spanish

▶ filling words from a box into gaps in a text.

In addition there will be a grammar test, where gapped sentences are given with a suggested verb, noun or adjective to fill the gaps. You will have to decide which form of the word to use.

Writing (35 marks)

Suggested time: 45 minutes

There will be a choice of three questions and you have to write one piece of at least 200 words in Spanish. The questions vary and you could be asked to write in various formats, such as a letter, an article, an essay or a report. All the titles are based on topics from the syllabus.

The key ways to prepare are by:
▶ learning key vocabulary for each topic area
▶ revising the main grammar points
▶ doing plenty of listening practice to keep your ear 'tuned in' to Spanish
▶ practising writing 200 word pieces in about 45 minutes
▶ working through the exam-type questions and tips on the following pages.

You are advised to allocate approximately 30 minutes for the Listening section. Check how many questions are involved, how the marks are allocated and use your time wisely.

Read the questions to see if the order helps you to work out the main structure or sequence of the listening task.

Think about the kind of information each question will require. Identify the main focus of the question word: where / who / when etc.

Whilst listening for the first time keep track of
▶ who is speaking
▶ what question you are on
▶ specific words or information you were expecting to hear.

For the second time of listening add all the relevant detail.
You can stop and repeat your own tape as often as you like so alternate between focusing on the overall sense of the passage and the detail you need to include.

Listening task 1 (Track 2)
Listen to this news item about a famous restaurant and provide the information required in English.

1) The restaurant's decision and its reasons. (3 marks)

2) The reactions of other people. (3 marks)

3) The owner's final response. (4 marks)

Un restaurante bastante famoso ha anunciado que piensa limitar la entrada a los mayores de dieciséis años, cosa que ha causado bastante crítica, no sin razón. El jefe de dicho lugar declaró que había gastado una fortuna en decorar su establecimiento y que los platos que servía no eran aptos para los menores de edad. Por esto pensaba que su decisión no era injusta.

La reacción a tal noticia ha sido bastante negativa y mucha gente se ha sorprendido sobre todo que en España suelen tolerar a los niños más fácilmente que en otras partes de Europa. Otros se preguntan que si es legal excluir a los menores y si existe una ley que proteja sus derechos.

La semana pasada el señor Ruiz respondió con una aclaración que decía que cualquier familia que quiera reservar tiene que indicar las edades de los hijos. Además insistía que la mayoría de sus clientes le apoyaban y aplaudían porque no les gustaba cenar con niños ruidosos al lado o alrededor.

Listening task 2 (Track 3)

Escucha la entrevista con tres adolescentes que hablan de la publicidad. Para cada frase escribe N (Nuria), P (Paco) o T (Teresa) para indicar la persona que habla.

1) Creo que <u>no se justifica</u> tentar a los niños de esta forma. ☐

2) <u>No hago caso de</u> la propaganda que ponen en la tele. ☐

3) Es bueno que pongan anuncios <u>útiles</u>. ☐

4) No había muchos anuncios en la tele cuando era <u>pequeña</u>. ☐

5) Me parece que hay que <u>proteger a los jóvenes</u>. ☐

6) A mí <u>me entretienen</u>, sobre todo los eslogans. ☐

Use your knowledge of synonyms to help you answer this sort of question. Often a word in the question is a synonym of a word on the recording and realising this helps you get the right answer.

When you have done the exercise, find the words in the transcript which mean more or less the same as the words or phrases which are underlined above.

Muchas veces nos quejamos de la cantidad de publicidad que hay dirigida precisamente a los niños. Hemos hablado de este tema con tres adolescentes para ver lo que opinan y cómo ha cambiado la cosa desde su niñez.

Bueno, Nuria ¿tú qué opinas de la publicidad para los niños hoy en día?

Pues, creo que ponen demasiada propaganda en la tele. Claro no me importa porque ya soy mayor y comprendo pero sé que a mi hermano pequeño le encanta y siempre pide en seguida los dulces o juguetes que han anunciado. Por eso creo que es malo y sé que no ponían tanta propaganda en la tele cuando yo era niña.

Vale, y tú, Paco ¿cuál es tu opinión?

Pues mi opinión es que es muy cruel anunciar toda clase de cosas interesantes para los niños y que luego no puedan comprarlas porque claro sus padres se oponen. Sin embargo a todos nos encanta la música, los colores y las voces tontas que usan. Todavía me acuerdo de los anuncios de cuando era niño.

Teresa ¿estás de acuerdo?

Depende – a mí me parece que hay anuncios en la tele que sí valen la pena por ejemplo los anuncios sobre comida sana. Pero cuando trata de un anuncio que no es apto para los niños o de golosinas y comida perjudicial entonces creo que no es justo y que debe haber más precauciones con la propaganda dirigida a los peques.

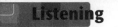

Listening task 3 (Track 4)

When you have a task which requires you to complete sentences by choosing from a list of words you will need to apply all the skills for listening and in particular use your knowledge of grammar to help you

▶ make sense of the word order

▶ make sense of the word order

▶ check for pronouns and other words used to refer back to things already mentioned without repetition

▶ be aware of negatives

▶ spot connecting words which indicate whether an idea is a continuation or a contrast

▶ determine the person and the tense of the verb.

Vuelta a España en patines
Escucha y completa la frase con una de las frases del recuadro.
¡Cuidado: sobran dos!

1) Pedro Márquez piensa dar la vuelta a España _____

2) Pasará _____

3) Tiene la intención de viajar unos 50 kilómetros _____

4) Ha adaptado sus patines para todos los _____

5) Espera completar su gira en _____

6) Va a ser acompañado por _____

cien días	34 años	en patines	terrenos
la noche	una caravana	27 provincias	diariamente

Pedro David Márquez comenzó en Vélez-Málaga en la costa del Sol a dar su vuelta al país en patines. Este madrileño de 34 años recorrerá 4.570 kilómetros pasando por las 27 provincias españolas, haciendo una media de 50 kilómetros diarios.
Lleva unos patines 'todo terreno' especiales y adaptables a las diferentes superficies que se va a encontrar en su camino: calles viejas o nuevas, parques o carreteras locales – encontrará de todo.
Cree que su recorrido va a durar unos cien días. Por supuesto habrá una caravana con coche que le seguirá y en donde podrá pasar la noche y recuperarse.

Listening task 4 (Track 5)

- Constantly revise whether you can make sense out of what you hear.
- If you have heard the sound of a word accurately, think carefully how it would be spelled in Spanish.
- Check if you have heard several words as one long word!
- Beware of false friends such as *realizar* (to achieve), *actual* (current), *sensible* (sensitive), *librería* (bookshop).
- Beware of words with two genders and two different meanings: *el capital* (sum of money) / *la capital* (city); *el policía* (policeman) / *la policía* (police force).

Escucha este anuncio sobre el parque nacional de la Doñana. Luego tienes que escoger la respuesta correcta para las cinco frases. Escribe A, B o C en la casilla.

Museo del mundo marino en Doñana

1) El museo se encuentra cerca de ⬚
  a) Gibraltar
  b) Cádiz
  c) Huelva

2) El objetivo del museo es de imitar ⬚
  a) el cielo
  b) el paisaje
  c) las joyas

3) Las dunas de la playa miden ⬚
  a) 30 metros de altura
  b) 3 metros de altura
  c) 300 metros de altura

4) La sala llamada La Mar incluye todo sobre ⬚
  a) los barcos
  b) el océano
  c) la pesca

5) La ecosfera fue desarrollada por la ⬚
  a) ONU
  b) NASA
  c) UE

Este museo situado en Matalascañas (Huelva) es un buen punto de partida para conocer la joya biológica de Doñana. Allí tratan de imitar el paisaje alrededor en salas cuyo nombre indica lo que contienen, por ejemplo, la primera sala, con dunas de 30 metros de altura, que se llama Las Dunas. Otras dos salas se acercan al visitante el medio marino se llaman una El Mar – sala que presenta los secretos del océano alrededor de la zona del Estrecho de Gibraltar – y la segunda La Mar – sala que trata de los pescadores y el arte de pescar. Una última sala, Barcos y Rutas, describe las vías transatlánticas que salieron de Huelva hacia las Américas.
Otro de los atractivos de este singular museo es la ecosfera, una tecnología desarrollada por la NASA que ha conseguido encerrar en una esfera de cristal una comunidad animal y vegetal autosuficiente, capaz de soportar viajes espaciales de larga duración.
Doñana es una de las zonas húmedas más importantes del mundo y es reconocida como Reserva de la Biosfera y Patrimonio Natural de la Humanidad.

Before you read look at:
▶ the layout – paragraphs, illustrations, titles and subtitles
▶ the subject or context, the main focus and what you expect to find there.
Scan through the whole text the first time you read it looking for key words and phrases.
Then select what appear to be key details for each of these on the second reading.
Learn to spot words which are there to fill out the sentence.
Make an educated guess from the context and words you already know.
Once you think you have the answer to each question use your knowledge of language to make a final check to make sure the answer works. For example be aware of negatives or tenses which may alter the meaning.

Reading task 1

Lee este texto y decide si las frases que siguen son verdaderas (V), falsas (F) o no se mencionan (N).

Tatuajes sin lágrimas

Los artistas de cine y ciertos personajes siempre han querido llamar la atención por su rebeldía. Ser rebelde o diferente nunca pasa de moda – solamente cambia la manera de expresarlo.

El problema antes era que a veces demostrar su rebeldía luciendo un tatuaje poco apropiado en una parte del cuerpo bastante visible tenía un resultado contrario al que se quería. Sin embargo hoy las estrellas han encontrado la forma perfecta de solucionar el problema de una manera bastante original: una marca de ropa que luce tatuajes.

Un modista francés está produciendo su propia marca de ropa callejera con diseños de un artista de tatuaje californiano – el famoso Don Ed Hardy. La gama del producto va desde zapatos y camisetas hasta bebidas isotónicas y todos los 'famosos y famosillas' la están comprando por miedo a quedarse fuera de onda.

1) La rebeldía es una marca importante para toda clase de personas.

2) La gente inventa muchas formas diferentes para expresar su rebeldía.

3) La forma de expresar su rebeldía no cambia nunca.

4) Los tatuajes siempre han sido un problema.

5) Lucir un tatuaje está mal visto.

6) A veces se pintan figuras muy vergonzosas en su cuerpo.

7) Las camisetas nuevas tienen cifras marcadas encima.

8) Los artistas se comprometen a ponerse la ropa callejera.

9) Don Hardy es una modista famosa de Francia.

10) La gente californiana está siempre de moda.

- Find names, numbers, dates or lists
- Look out for words that appear regularly
- Break down words – prefixes, suffixes, verb endings
- Check the role of the word in the sentence
- Think of similar words or phrases which could be used as an alternative in Spanish
- Think about how you can change the word order or parts of speech
- Change passive sentences in English into active ones in Spanish
- Be prepared to define or explain

Reading task 2
Lee el artículo y contesta a las preguntas.

Homenaje a las víctimas
Fantasmas del pasado resurgen de nuevo para dividir a los españoles. En Las Cortes han hecho homenaje a centenares de prisioneros políticos, a fusilados y exiliados y a las brigadas internacionales. Entregaron certificados reconociendo su 'lucha por la libertad'. Un portavoz declaró que 'se puede perdonar pero no olvidar y queremos honrar a todos sin ofender a nadie'. Sin embargo hay muchos que también quieren condenar la rebelión de 1936 encabezada por Franco y sus generales que llevó al país a 40 años de régimen totalitario.

Hace dos años aprobaron una propuesta parlamentaria que reconocía por primera vez la existencia de víctimas de la dictadura. De hecho, las CC.AA. estaban libres para rescatar los cadáveres de miles de víctimas que se suponen estén aún sepultados en una fosa común sin marcar.

La transición a la democracia tuvo éxito en parte gracias a 'el pacto del olvido' por ambos lados. Por eso existen muchas historias que hasta ahora no se han contado. No obstante, hace poco el debate ha resucitado de nuevo con acusaciones y maldicciones.

Los historiadores siguen discutiendo las cifras verdaderas de aquel conflicto. Sea el número que sea, la gente aún estará dividida.

1) ¿De qué período histórico trata el texto?

2) ¿Quiénes son las fantasmas del pasado?

3) ¿Qué pasó hace dos años?

4) ¿Cuál fue el resultado de este evento?

5) Explica lo que significa 'el pacto del olvido'.

Reading task 3

Aqui tienes un artículo sobre las presiones a las que se enfrentan los jóvenes hoy en día. Rellena los espacios en el texto con las palabras del recuadro. Usa cada palabra una sola vez. Sobran cuatro palabras.

llegar	bonita	para	permitir
quieren	nuevo	importante	apariencia
sobre	cierto	de	mucho

La pregunta: ¿Crees que hay demasiadas presiones sobre los jóvenes hoy en día?

Las respuestas:

Pedro

Sí, hay muchas sobre todo cuando se trata de 'ser aceptados' por los amigos. Creo que soy bastante fuerte de carácter pero me gusta ponerme ropa (1) _____ sobre todo cuando salgo en pandilla. Sin embargo juego con un equipo de baloncesto y practico los fines de semana de modo que no tengo (2) _____ tiempo se salir de noche. Además creo que en el cole sería mejor llevar uniforme para no tener ese problema.

Susana

Pues yo sí tengo algunos problemas porque mis padres no me dejan salir si no es con mi hermano mayor. Creo que mis padres deben (3) _____ que yo salga por lo menos los sábados en grupo. Tengo dieciséis años y ellos no (4) _____ aceptar que tenga mis propias ideas. He pensado mucho sobre este problema y me parece que es muy (5) _____ que me dejen desarrollar mi personalidad a mi manera.

Enrique

Bueno, en mi opinión es necesario tener bastante confianza en ti mismo hoy en día porque las revistas y todo el mundo te aconsejan sobre tu (6) _____ personal. Insisten que te vistas de cierta forma o que te pongas (7) _____ tipo de zapatos. Para mí lo más importante es decidir lo que tú quieres hacer en la vida y no hacer caso (8) _____ las presiones estúpidas de la moda, de las adicciones los amigos tontos.

- ▶ Use your knowledge of grammar to help you. Gaps 1 and 2 are both adjectives, but the first must be feminine singular and the second masculine singular. For gap 3 you need a word to follow 'deben' so you know you are looking for an infinitive. Gap 8 requires a preposition to follow the verb.
- ▶ Think too about what makes sense. What is likely to fit in gap 4: 'My parents don't _____ to accept that I have my own ideas'. Or in gap 6, which must be a noun.

When you are asked to match up two pieces of information follow all the previous tips for reading, scanning etc. a text.

Then in particular look out for cognates or near cognates (words of similar meanings) first.

Check whether there are any phrases in the information which are summed up in one word in the matching part of the task.

Look for opposites (antonyms) or negatives in one section which reflect the meaning in another.

Discard non-essential language which can confuse the issue.

Reading task 4

En una entrevista el guitarrista Paco Peña dio estas respuestas.
Primero lee las respuestas.

1) Pues paso horas practicando y buscando mejorar mi música. Es que soy perfeccionista pero en realidad no sufro porque al final sé que he triunfado y he superado el reto de perfeccionar mi estilo.

2) Lo más grave de todo sería si la música comenzara a perder su individualidad. Lo que pasa es que la música que se oye a menudo hoy parece toda igual. Cuando se aprecia y respeta la tradición cultural propia, la música es más genuina.

3) Me acuerdo bien. Fue cuando cogí por instinto la guitarra de mi hermano mayor. Eramos nueve en mi casa y siempre sonaba la música por todas partes.

4) A mi modo de ver, el flamenco es la forma más profunda y exquisita de expresar el arte en la música. La canción flamenca del gran cantante Camarón de la Isla no tiene igual con su intensidad y dulzura a partes iguales.

5) Fue cuando decidí formar el grupo de quince personas. Quería realizar mis sueños y poner en práctica mis ideas y fue el momento apropiado para hacerlo.

6) Me parece que aquí, dentro de una variedad interesante, existe más conformismo, mientras que en mi país los músicos buscan la aventura y están dispuestos a experimentar más y arriesgarse con la forma.

7) Cuando tenía 24 años decidí que quería ser solista y me fui a Londres porque en la España de entonces los guitarristas flamencos siempre tocaban en grupo, no a solas. Un año más tarde ya tocaba con Jimi Hendrix en el Albert Hall.

8) Pues sí y no. Por un lado no he tenido tiempo para mucho salvo mi música. Suelo practicar durante horas y por eso tengo que admitir que mi mujer ha sufrido bastante en el sentido de no tener un esposo de tiempo completo.

9) Cuando comencé a tocar como solista me ofrecieron bastante dinero para ser parte del famoso grupo Los Gypsy Kings pero me negué. Fue

un momento bastante traumático pero creo que fue una decisión acertada a fin de cuentas.

10) Claro que sí; cuando se tocan las emociones con la música se vuelven más vulnerables y a la vez más receptivas a todo lo que pasa a su alrededor.

11) A todos les aconsejaría buscar la belleza en la tradición y evitar la satisfacción momentánea de lo que es nuevo. Lo moderno no siempre es lo mejor.

Ahora lee las preguntas del entrevistador.
Decide cuál es la mejor pregunta para cada respuesta. Pon el número apropiado en cada casilla.
¡Cuidado! Sólo vas a usar 10 de las 11 respuestas de la lista y sólo vas a usar cada respuesta **una** vez.

a) ¿Cuál es su primer recuerdo de la música?

b) ¿Cómo comenzó su carrera?

c) ¿Cuál es su característica más impresionante?

d) ¿Ha hecho algunos sacrificios en su vida?

e) ¿Cuál ha sido la decisión más importante en su vida?

f) ¿Qué consejos le daría a un músico jóven al comienzo de su carrera?

g) En su opinión ¿cuál es la amenaza más seria para la música hoy en día?

h) ¿Cómo se compara la escena musical de Inglaterra con la de España?

i) ¿Cuál ha sido el momento clave en su vida?

j) ¿Cree usted que la música puede cambiar el mundo?

Answer the questions in Spanish.

Don't focus on the stimulus material only
Read the question carefully
Note the specific points required
Give your personal reaction and explain why
Include some factual knowledge
Make reference to the Spanish-speaking world

Think about how to present your answer:
▶ as a letter or email
▶ as a structured and reasoned argument
▶ as an imaginative response.

Make a clear plan:
▶ an introduction – respond to the question
▶ a list of points or series of ideas for paragraphs
▶ add facts, explanations, justifications for each one.

Conclusion – sum up concisely what you have written, but try not to repeat exactly the same words and phrases.

Jot down
▶ some prepared phrases for presenting ideas
▶ some prepared phrases for showing off language structures
▶ some connecting or contrasting words.

Check your work and make sure
▶ it follows a logical sequence
▶ it sticks to the point
▶ verb endings are correct
▶ adjectives agree
▶ accents are correctly placed.

Here are some sample questions.

Media (Advertising)
¿Crees que se debe prohibir la propaganda dirigida hacia los niños?

Popular Culture

Los adolescentes de hoy en día son como ovejas – siguen en rebanõ el ejemplo del líder en cuanto a su apariencia, sus hábitos, sus gustos – en fin, en todo lo que hacen.

Healthy Living / lifestyle

El problema de la obesidad es el más inquietante de todos los problemas de salud.

Family / Relationships

Jamás debes delatar a tu mejor amigo/a. Chivarse es lo peor. Tu mejor amigo/a es de por vida no importa lo que haga.

Los jóvenes no reciben el apoyo necesario ni del estado ni de la familia ni del instituto.

Assessment criteria

Each question will be marked out of 35. You will be given 20 marks for content and 15 marks for quality of language.

20 marks for Content

17–20 = Very good. Fully relevant response in depth; well organised structure and logical sequence; points well expressed and justified.

1–4 = Poor. Limited response and very little information; no real structure; points difficult to understand; little or no justification.

15 marks for Quality of Language

5 marks for Range of Vocabulary: 5 = wide and appropriate range; 1 = very little appropriate vocabulary.

5 marks for Structures: 5 = very good variety of grammar; 1 = little grasp of grammar.

5 marks for Accuracy: 5 = any inaccuracies only in complex language; 1 = errors make it hard to understand.

1 Nouns and determiners

Nouns are the words used to name people, animals, places, objects and ideas.

1.1 Gender: masculine and feminine

All nouns in Spanish are either masculine or feminine.

Endings of nouns **often but not always** indicate their gender. Many of the exceptions are fairly common words.

Masculine endings
-o, -e, -i, -u, -or

Exceptions
la radio (radio), *la calle* (street), *la tribu* (tribe), *la flor* (flower)

Feminine endings
-a, -ión, -ad, -z, -is, -ie, -umbre, -nza, -cia

Exceptions
el poeta (poet), *el avión* (aeroplane), *el pez* (fish), *el pie* (foot)

1. **List the other categories for masculine and feminine nouns.**

▶ Some nouns have two genders and two meanings:
el corte (cut of hair or suit); *la corte* (the royal court)

2. **Write a list of the most common two-gender words and their meanings.**

1.2 Singular and plural

To form the plural:
Add -s to nouns ending in a vowel
el libro (book) → *los libros*; *la regla* (ruler) → *las reglas*; *el café* (café) → *los cafés*
Add -es to nouns ending in a consonant
el hotel (hotel) → *los hoteles*; *el profesor* (teacher) → *los profesores*
except for words ending in -s, which do not change in the plural
el lunes (Monday) → *los lunes*; *la crisis* (crisis) → *las crisis*

▶ Words that end in -z change this to c and add -es:
la nariz (nose) → *las narices*

▶ Some nouns are used only in the plural:
las gafas (spectacles)

3. **Write the plural for kings, parents, homework, pencils, Tuesdays.**

1.3 Determiners: definite and indefinite articles

Determiners such as the **definite article (the)** and the **indefinite article (a / an, some, any)** are used with nouns and can tell you whether the noun is masculine (m.), feminine (f.), singular (sing.) or plural (pl.).

Note: Feminine words which begin with a stressed *a* or *ha* take *el / un* because it makes them easier to pronounce, but they still need a feminine adjective:

El agua está fría. (The water is cold.)
el hambre (hunger) but *Tengo mucha hambre.* (I'm very hungry.)
This use of *el / un* does not apply if the noun has an adjective before it:
la fría agua.

▶ Use the definite article with parts of the body and clothes, with languages – but not after *hablar* (to speak), *estudiar* (to study) or *saber* (to know) – with mountains, seas and rivers, and with certain countries and cities and people's official titles.

(4) When is the article NOT used?

▶ When *a* or *de* comes before *el* then a single word is formed:
a + el → al, de + el → del

1.4 The neuter article *lo*

This is used with an adjective to make an abstract noun.
Lo bueno es que ... (The good thing [about it] is ...)

1.5 Demonstrative adjectives and pronouns are used to point out an object or person.

singular		plural	
m.	f.	m.	f.
este	esta	estos	estas
ese	esa	esos	esas
aquel	aquella	aquellos	aquellas

Demonstrative pronouns take an accent and agree with the noun they are replacing. They **never** have a definite or indefinite article before them.

éste	ésta	éstos	éstas
ése	ésa	ésos	ésas
aquél	aquélla	aquéllos	aquéllas

Note: The forms *esto* and *eso* refer to general ideas or unknown things.

(5) Say what each one means: *este, ese, aquel*.

1.6 Possessive adjectives and pronouns

Possessive **adjectives** show who or what something belongs to.

singular		plural		
m.	**f.**	**m.**	**f.**	
mi	mi	mis	mis	my
tu	tu	tus	tus	your
su	su	sus	sus	his / her / your (formal)
nuestro	nuestra	nuestros	nuestras	our
vuestro	vuestra	vuestros	vuestras	your
su	su	sus	sus	their / your plural (formal)

Remember to use the definite article rather than a possessive adjective with parts of the body and clothes:

Voy a lavarme el pelo. (I'm going to wash my hair.)

Possessive **pronouns** are used instead of the noun. They **do have** a definite article before them.

singular		plural	
m.	**f.**	**m.**	**f.**
el mío	la mía	los míos	las mías
el tuyo	la tuya	los tuyos	las tuyas
el suyo	la suya	los suyos	las suyas
el nuestro	la nuestra	los nuestros	las nuestras
el vuestro	la vuestra	los vuestros	las vuestras
el suyo	la suya	los suyos	las suyas

Other determiners are:

indefinite adjectives or pronouns and quantifiers:

some(one), some(thing), any, each, other, another
otro día, otra persona, alguno (algún), alguna, todo, mucho

6 Translate: I'm going to wash my hair. Your t-shirt is nicer than mine. The ham sandwich is yours and mine is the cheese. Their house is bigger than ours.

2 Adjectives

Adjectives are the words used to describe nouns.

2.1 Making adjectives agree

In English the adjective always stays the same. In Spanish it changes to agree with the word it is describing according to whether this is masculine, feminine or plural.

▶ Adjectives ending in *-o* (masculine) change to *-a* for the feminine form: *bonito* (pretty) → *bonita*

▶ Many other adjectives have a common form for masculine and feminine: *un loro verde* (a green parrot) / *una culebra verde* (a green snake) → *unos loros verdes* / *unas culebras verdes*

▶ Adjectives ending in *-or* add *-a* for the feminine form: *hablador* (talkative) → *habladora*

▶ Adjectives ending in *-án*, *-ón* and *-ín* add *-a* for the feminine form and lose their accent: *holgazán* (lazy) → *holgazana*

▶ To make an adjective plural, follow the same rule as for nouns.

Add *-s* to a vowel: *unos pájaros rojos* (some red birds), *unas tortugas pequeñas* (some small tortoises)

Add *-es* to a consonant: *unos ratones grises* (some grey mice), *unos perros jóvenes* (some young dogs)

Change *-z* to *-ces*: *un ave rapaz* (a bird of prey) → *unas aves rapaces*

▶ Some adjectives of colour never change: *el vestido rosa* (the pink dress), *el jersey naranja* (the orange jumper)

▶ When an adjective describes two or more masculine nouns or a mixture of masculine and feminine nouns, usually the masculine plural form is used.

▶ If the adjective comes before more than one noun it tends to agree with the first noun:

Tiene una pequeña casa y coche (She has a small house and car.)

2.2 Shortened adjectives

Some adjectives lose their final *-o* before a masculine singular noun. *buen, mal, primer, tercer, ningún, algún*

▶ Any compound of *-un* shortens also:
Hay veintiún chicos en la clase.
(There are twenty-one children in the class.)

▶ *grande* and *cualquiera* shorten before both masculine and feminine nouns:
Es un gran hombre. (He is a great man.)
Cualquier día llegará. (It will arrive some day.)

▶ *ciento* shortens to *cien* before **all** nouns (see section 19).

(7) Write further examples of your own for all the points made above.

2.3 Position of adjectives

In Spanish, adjectives usually come **after** the noun:
Mi hermana pequeña tiene un gato negro. (My little sister has a black cat.)

Numbers, possessive adjectives and qualifiers come before nouns:
mi primer día en el cole (my first day at school); *cada día* (every day);
poca gente (few people)

▶ Sometimes whether an adjective is positioned before or after the
  noun affects its meaning.
  un gran hombre = a great man, but *un hombre grande* = a tall man

(8) Make a list of the other adjectives which vary in this way.

3 Adverbs

Adverbs are used to describe the action of a verb. They can also describe
adjectives or another adverb. In English they often end in '-ly'.

▶ Many adverbs are formed by adding *-mente* to an adjective:
  fácil → *fácilmente* (easily); *posible* → *posiblemente* (possibly)

▶ If the adjective has a different feminine form, you add *-mente* to this:
  lento → *lenta* + *-mente* = *lentamente* (slowly)

▶ Sometimes it is better to use a preposition and a noun:
  con frecuencia (frequently), *con cuidado* (carefully)

▶ Sometimes, as in English, an adjective can also be used as an adverb,
  e.g. *duro* (hard)

▶ Some adverbs do not end in *-mente*: *siempre* (always), *nunca* (never),
  muy (very), *mucho* (much, a lot), *poco* (little, not very much), *bastante*
  (enough) and *demasiado* (too much) can be either adjectives or
  adverbs.

▶ When two or more adverbs are used together then only the last one
  has *-mente* added to it:
  El ladrón entró cautelosa, silenciosa y lentamente.
  (The robber entered cautiously, silently and slowly)

(9) Write other adverbs to illustrate each of the points made above.

4 Comparisons

Adjectives and adverbs follow the same rules.

4.1 The comparative

To compare one thing, person or idea with another in Spanish use:
más + adjective / adverb + *que*
menos + adjective / adverb + *que*

▶ When *más* or *menos* is used with a number or a quantity, *de* is used in place of *que*.

▶ To say one thing is similar to or the same as another, you can use: *el mismo que / la misma que* (the same as); *tan ... como* (as ... as); *tanto ... como* (as much ... as)

▶ To say 'the more ... the more ...' use: *cuanto más ... (tanto) más ...*

▶ To say 'the less ... the less ...' use: *cuanto menos ... (tanto) menos ...*

4.2 The superlative

The superlative compares one thing, person or idea with several others. To make a superlative, use:
el / la / los / las más (the most); *el / la / los / las menos* (the least)
el / la mejor, los / las mejores (the best); *el / la peor, los / las peores* (the worst)

Las películas de terror son las menos divertidas de todas.
(Horror films are the least entertaining of all.)

▶ If the superlative adjective immediately follows the noun you leave out *el / la / los / las*:
Es el río más largo del mundo. (It is the longest river in the world.)

▶ Note that *de* translates 'in' after a superlative.

▶ Absolute superlatives -*ísimo* / -*ísima* / -*ísimos* / -*ísimas* – are added to adjectives to give emphasis and express a high degree of something.

Tengo muchísimas ganas de verte.
(I'm looking forward to seeing you so very much.)
La comida fue rica – pero riquísima.
(The meal was delicious – absolutely delicious.)

Irregular forms of the comparative and superlative
These do not have different masculine and feminine forms:
mejor: el mejor / la mejor (the best)
peor: el peor / la peor (the worst)

mayor and *menor*, meaning 'older' and 'younger', can also be used to mean 'bigger' and 'smaller'.

(10) **Write five comparisons about your favourite TV programmes.**

5 Prepositions and linking words

5.1 Prepositions

Prepositions are used before nouns, noun phrases and pronouns, usually indicating where a person or object is.

▶ Verbs following a preposition in Spanish must be in the infinitive form:
después de entrar (after entering); *al volver a casa* (on returning home)
Some common uses:

▶ *a* = direction or movement to / at a specific point in time

▶ *en* = 'in' or 'on' or sometimes 'by'

▶ Many other prepositions are followed by *de*:
delante de (in front of); *detrás de* (behind); *al lado de* (next to)

Remember: *a* + *el* = *al*; *de* + *el* = *del*.

(11) Write down examples for each usage.

▶ Both *por* and *para* are usually translated by 'for' in English, but they have different uses:
por = 'along' / 'through'; 'by' / how; in exchange for something; a period or length of time; cause. It is also used with the passive:
hecho por los Romanos (made by the Romans)

para = who or what something is for; purpose; 'in order to'; future time

(12) Find some useful expressions containing *por* and *para*.

▶ Personal *a*

This is not translated into English, but is used before object pronouns and nouns referring to specific and defined people and animals. It is a mark of respect to distinguish living things from objects.
Busco a mi hermano. (I am looking for my brother.)
Quiero a mis abuelos. (I love my grandparents.)
Pregunta a tu profe. (Ask your teacher.)
It is not used after *tener*: *Tengo un hermano y dos primas.*
(I have one brother and two girl cousins.)
It is not used if the person is not yet specified:
Se busca joven dependiente. (Young salesperson sought.)

(13) Translate: I have a younger brother and I love my older sister.

5.2 Conjunctions – link words (connectives)

These are used to connect words, phrases and clauses.
y (and), *o* (or), *ni* (neither), *pero* (but), *sino* (but)

(14) When does *y* change to *e* and *o* to *u*?

▶ *pero* and *sino* both mean 'but'.

(15) Write two sentences to illustrate the difference.

6 Pronouns

A pronoun is a word that can be used instead of a noun, an idea or even a whole phrase. It helps to avoid repetition.

6.1 Subject pronouns

yo	I	*nosotros/as*	we
tú	you sing. (informal)	*vosotros/as*	you pl. (informal)
él, ella, usted	he, she, you (formal)	*ellos, ellas, ustedes*	they (m, f), pl. (formal)

Grammar Summary

▶ The subject pronouns are not often used in Spanish as the verb ending generally indicates the subject of the verb. You might use them for emphasis or to avoid ambiguity.

▶ To refer to a group of people with one or more males in it, use the masculine plural form.

6.2 Tú and usted, vosotros/as and ustedes

are the four ways of saying 'you' in Spanish.

(16) Write definitions for each one.

6.3 Reflexive pronouns

Reflexive pronouns – *me, te, se, nos, os, se* – are used to form reflexive verbs and refer back to the subject of the verb (see section 12).
They are often not translated into English:
Me levanto a las siete y me ducho. (I get up at seven and shower.)

6.4 Direct object pronouns

Direct object pronouns – *me, te, le / lo / la, nos, os, les / los / las* – are used for the person or thing directly affected by the action of the verb. They replace a noun that is the object of a verb.

¿Tus gafas? Las pusiste en tu bolso para no olvidarlas.
(Your glasses? You put them in your bag so as not to forget them.)

(17) Follow the example and write two more.

6.5 Indirect object pronouns

An indirect object pronoun replaces a noun (usually a person) that is linked to the verb by a preposition, usually *a* ('to').
Te toca a ti (It's your turn)

▶ You also use them to refer to parts of the body.
Me duelen los oídos. (My ears ache / I've got earache.)

▶ When there are several pronouns in the same sentence and linked to the same verb they go in this order:
reflexive – indirect object – direct object (R.I.D.)

6.6 Two pronouns together

When two pronouns beginning with l *(le / lo / la / les / los / las)* come together then the indirect object pronoun changes to *se (se lo / se la / se los / se las)*.
Quiero regalar un libro a mi padre. (I want to give a book to my father.)
Se lo quiero regalar. / Quiero regalárselo.
(I want to give it to him. / I want to give him it.)

(18) Translate: I want to give her a book. No, Pepe wants to give it to her.

6.7 Position of pronouns

Reflexive, direct object and indirect object pronouns usually

▶ immediately precede the verb:
No la veo. (I can't see her.)
Se llama Lucía. (She's called Lucy.)
Te doy mil euros. (I'll give you a thousand euros.)

▶ attach to the end of the infinitive, present participle or positive command:
Voy a verla mañana. (I'm going to see her tomorrow.)
Tengo que levantarme temprano. (I've got to get up early.)
Estoy mirándolo ahora. (I'm looking at it now.)
Está bañándose. (She's bathing.)
Levantaos enseguida. (Get up at once.)
Dámelo. (Give me it.)
However, it is now widely accepted to put them before the infinitive or the present participle.

For possessive pronouns see section 1.6.

(19) Translate: He has to get up early tomorrow. Go away (four different versions). I am watching her. Give them it now.

6.8 Disjunctive pronouns (emphatic pronouns)

These are used after a preposition (see section 4):
para mí (for me); *hacia ti* (towards you); *junto a él / ella / usted* (next to him / her / you); *detrás de nosotros/as* (behind us); *entre vosotros/as* (between yourselves); *cerca de ellos / ellas / ustedes* (near to them / you)

▶ Remember with *con* (with) to use *conmigo* (with me), *contigo* (with you), *consigo* (with him[self] / with her[self] / with one[self]).

(20) Write sentences to illustrate each one.

6.9 Relative pronouns and adjectives

Some of these are determiners as well. They link two parts of a sentence.

▶ The relative pronoun *que* ('who', 'which' or 'that') is always used in Spanish and not left out of the sentence as it often is in English.
Ese es el vestido que me gusta. (That is the dress [that] I like.)
Señala a la persona que habla. (Point to the person [who is] speaking.)

▶ After the prepositions *a, de, con* and *en* use *que* for things and *quien / quienes* for people.

▶ After other prepositions use *el cual, la cual, los cuales, las cuales.*

▶ *cuyo / cuya / cuyos / cuyas* are used to mean 'whose' and are best treated as an adjective as they agree with the noun they refer to.

Mi madre, cuyos perros no me gustan, va conmigo.

(My mother, whose dogs I don't like, is going with me).
For demonstrative pronouns see section 1.5; see section 1.6 for possessive pronouns.

(21) Translate: That's the dress I like. Jim is a student I work with.

6.10 Neuter pronouns

eso and *ello* refer to something unspecific such as an idea or fact:
No me hables más de eso. (Don't talk to me any more about that.)
No quiero pensar jamás en ello. (I don't ever want to think about it.)

▶ *lo que / lo cual* are relative pronouns; they refer to a general idea or phrase rather than a specific noun:
Ayer hubo una huelga de Correos, lo cual me molestó mucho.
(Yesterday there was a postal strike, which caused me a lot of bother.)

7 Interrogatives and exclamations

7.1 Direct questions and exclamations

(22) What is the rule for writing questions and exclamations in Spanish?

▶ Make your voice rise slightly at the start when asking a question.

▶ Here are some common question words and exclamation words. Note that they all have accents:

¿Qué? ¿Por qué? ¿Cuándo? ¿Cómo? ¿Dónde? ¿Adónde? ¿Quién? ¿Quiénes? ¿Cuál? ¿Cuáles? ¿Cuánto? / ¿Cuánta? ¿Cuántos? / ¿Cuántas? ¡Qué! ¡Cómo! ¡Cuánto/a(s)!

7.2 Indirect questions and exclamations

▶ Indirect question words and exclamations also take an accent:
No me dijo a qué hora iba a llegar.
(He didn't tell me when he was going to arrive.)
No sabes cómo y cuánto lo siento. (You don't know how sorry I am.)

8 Negatives

You can make a statement negative in Spanish simply by putting *no* before the verb:
No quiero salir. (I don't want to go out.)
No me gusta la historia. (I don't like history.)

▶ Some other common negatives are:
ninguno / (ningún) / ninguna (no [adjective]); *nada* (nothing); *nadie* (nobody); *nunca / jamás* (never); *ni ... ni ...* (neither ... nor); *tampoco* (neither [negative of *también*])

▶ If any of these words is used after the verb, you have to use *no* as well. But if the negative word comes **before** the verb, *no* is not needed:
No he fumado nunca. / Nunca he fumado. (I've never smoked.)

▶ You can use several negatives in a sentence in Spanish:
Nadie sabía nada acerca de ninguno de ellos.
(Nobody knew anything about any of them.)

(23) Write sentences about something you dislike to illustrate all the negatives.

9 Verbs: the indicative mood

A verb indicates **what** is happening (an action or a state) in a sentence and the tense indicates **when**.

9.1 The infinitive

In a dictionary verbs are listed in the infinitive form. In Spanish verbs are grouped according to the last two letters of the infinitive:
-ar: comprar (to buy)   *-er: comer* (to eat)   *-ir: subir* (to go up)

▶ The infinitive itself is often used after another verb. Common verbs usually followed by an infinitive are: *querer, gustar, poder, tener que, deber.*

▶ *Soler,* used only in the present and imperfect tenses, indicates what usually happens:
Suelo levantarme temprano. (I usually get up early.)
¿Qué solías hacer cuando eras joven, abuela?
(What did you use to do when you were young, Grandma?)

▶ The infinitive is also used in impersonal commands or instructions:
No entrar (Do not enter)
and as a noun:
Estudiar es duro cuando hace calor. (Studying is hard when it's hot.)
For verbs which take *a* or *de* + infinitive, see section 18.1.
The infinitive also follows prepositions: see section 18.2.
For the past infinitive see section 9.9.

9.2 The present tense

Regular verbs			Reflexive verbs
comprar	***comer***	***subir***	***levantarse***
compro	*como*	*subo*	*me levanto*
compras	*comes*	*subes*	*te levantas*
compra	*come*	*sube*	*se levanta*
compramos	*comemos*	*subimos*	*nos levantamos*
compráis	*coméis*	*subís*	*os levantáis*
compran	*comen*	*suben*	*se levantan*

▶ Some verbs change their spelling to preserve the same sound as in the infinitive:

g before *e* or *i* changes to *j* before *a*, *o* or *u*: *coger – cojo, coges, coge* etc.

gu before *e* or *i* changes to *g* before *a*, *o* or *u*: *seguir – sigo, sigues, sigue* etc.

▶ Some verbs need to add a written accent:
continuar – continúo, continúas, continúa
enviar – envío, envías, envía etc.

▶ Radical changes – where the stem of the verb changes when stressed:
o →*ue*: *contar – cuento, cuentas, cuenta, contamos, contáis, cuentan*
  dormir – duermo, duermes, duerme, dormimos, dormís, duermen
u →*ue*: *jugar – juego, juegas, juega, jugamos, jugáis, juegan*
e →*i*: *empezar – empiezo, empiezas, empieza, empezamos, empezáis, empiezan*
e →*i*: *pedir – pido, pides, pide, pedimos, pedís, piden*

(24) **Write sentences to illustrate each of the spelling changes and radical changes listed.**

▶ Irregular verbs – the five most common you will need are:
ser (to be); *estar* (to be); *ir* (to go); *tener* (to have); *hacer* (to do).

(25) **Make up a mnemonic to remember these five verbs.**

Some verbs are only irregular in the first person of the present tense, then follow the regular pattern:
poner – pongo, pones etc.
salir – salgo, sales etc.
conducir – conduzco, conduces etc.
See the verb table on page 48.
Note: *hay* = 'there is' / 'there are'

▶ Use the present tense

 – to describe what is happening now or what regularly happens, a repeated action or habit;
 – to refer to something that started in the past and continues into the present:
Vivo aquí desde hace años. (I've been living here for years.)
 – to express the future:
Adiós. Nos vemos mañana. (Goodbye. We'll see each other tomorrow.)

9.3 The present continuous

Use the present tense of *estar* and the present participle of the main verb formed as follows:
-ar → *-ando*, *-er* → *-iendo*, *-ir* → *-iendo*
Exceptions include: *leyendo* (reading) and *durmiendo* (sleeping).

▶ It indicates what is happening at the time of speaking or that one action is happening at the same time as another. It follows the English pattern closely.

▶ It is often used with *pasar* to express how you spend time:

Paso el tiempo divirtiéndome, mirando la tele, haciendo deporte.
(I spend the time amusing myself, watching the TV, doing sport.)

▶ It is also often used after *seguir, ir and llevar.*

9.4 The preterite tense

This is formed by adding the following endings to the stem of the verb:

-ar:	*-é, -aste, -ó, -amos, -asteis, -aron*
-er, -ir:	*-í, -iste, -ió, -imos, -isteis, -ieron*

(26) Write out the regular verbs *comprar, comer, subir* in full.

▶ Spelling changes
Some verbs change their spelling to preserve the same sound as in the infinitive:

c → qu before *e: sacar – sa**qu**é, sacaste, sacó* etc.
g → gu before *e: pagar – pa**gu**é, pagaste, pagó* etc.
i → y between two vowels: *creer – creí, creíste, cre**y**ó, creímos, creísteis, cre**y**eron* (also *leer, oír, caer*)
gu → gü before *e: averiguar – aver**gü**é, averiguaste, averguó* etc.
Conversely, *z*, which is required before *a* or *o*, reverts to *c* before *e*:
*empezar – empe**c**é, empezaste, empezó* etc.

▶ Radical changes
-ir verbs change in the third person singular and plural:

*o → u: morir – m**u**rió, m**u**rieron* (also *dormir*)
*e → i: pedir – p**i**dió, p**i**dieron* (also *sentir, mentir, seguir, vestir*)

(27) Write sentences to illustrate each of the above changes.

▶ Some common irregular verbs. Note that there are no accents.
It helps to learn irregulars in groups; some follow a pattern of *uve*:

andar anduve etc.	*estar estuve* etc.	*tener tuve* etc.

Note *ser* and *ir* have the same form so *fui* can mean either
'I went' or 'I was'.
fui, fuiste, fue, fuimos, fuisteis, fueron
dar and *ver* follow a similar pattern.
dar – di, diste, dio, dimos, disteis, dieron
ver – vi, viste, vio, vimos, visteis, vieron
A larger group are quite irregular:

hacer	**haber**	**poder**	**poner**	**querer**	**venir**
hice	*hube*	*pude*	*puse*	*quise*	*vine*

(28) Write all the persons for each irregular verb started above.

▶ Use the preterite

– to refer to events, actions and states started and completed in the past:
El año pasado hubo una huelga de los empleados del metro.
(Last year there was a strike on the Underground.)
– to refer to events, actions or states which took place over a defined period of time but are now completed:
Mis padres vivieron en Guatemala durante tres años.
(My parents lived in Guatemala for three years.)

9.5 The imperfect tense

This is formed by adding the following endings to the stem:
-ar: *-aba, -abas, -aba, -ábamos, -abais, -aban*
-er / -ir: *-ía, -ías, -ía, -íamos, -íais, -ían*
There are only three irregular verbs: *ir, ser* and *ver.*

(29) **Write out the full forms for the following verbs:**
comprar, comer, subir, ir, ser, ver.

▶ Use the imperfect tense:

– to indicate what used to happen (a regular or repeated action in the past
– to say what happened over a long (indefinite) period of time
– to say what was happening (a continuous action)
– to describe what someone or something was like in the past
– to describe or set the scene in a narrative in the past
– in expressions of time (where English would use a pluperfect):

Acababa de llegar cuando tuvo una sorpresa grande.
(He had just arrived when he got a big surprise.)
Esperaba su respuesta desde hacía más de un mes.
(He had been waiting for her reply for more than a month.)
– to make a polite request:
Quería pedirte un gran favor.
(I would like to ask you a big favour.)

9.6 The imperfect continuous

This is formed by taking the imperfect form of estar – estaba – and adding the present participle.

¿Qué estabas haciendo? Estaba bañándome.
(What were you doing? I was bathing.)
Just like the present continuous it indicates what was happening at a particular moment – in this case in the past.
It is also used to describe an action interrupted by another action:
Estaba leyendo el periódico cuando llegó el correo.
(I was reading the newspaper when the post arrived.)

(30) **Translate: I had just arrived when it started to rain. It rained all day and when I was running home it suddenly stopped raining and the sun came out.**

9.7 The future tense

This is formed by taking the infinitive of regular verbs and adding the following endings:
-é, -ás, -á, -emos, -éis, -án
Irregular verbs take the same future endings as regular ones – the irregularity lies in the stem.

comprar	comer	subir
compraré	*comeré*	*subiré*

Some common irregulars

decir → diré	*haber → habré*	*hacer → haré*	*poder → podré*
poner → pondré	*querer → querré*	*saber → sabré*	*salir → saldré*
tener → tendre	*venir → vendré*		

▶ Use the future to:
- indicate what will happen or take place
- express an obligation
- express a supposition, probability or surprise.

If you want to express willingness or a request use *querer*:
¿Quieres decirlo otra vez? (Would you like to say that again?)

9.8 The immediate future

Another way to indicate what is going to happen is to take the verb *ir + a* and add the infinitive.
Voy a escribir una carta. (I'm going to write a letter.)
¿A qué hora vas a venir? (When are you going to come?)

(31) Write a few sentences about what you are going to do next week and what you will do later in the term.

9.9 The conditional tense

This is formed by taking the infinitive of regular verbs and adding the following endings:
-ía, -ías, -ía, -íamos, -íais, -ían

Irregular verbs have the same conditional endings as regular ones – the irregularity lies in the stem, just as for the future tense (see 9.7 above).

▶ Use the conditional:
- to indicate what would, could or should happen
- in 'if' clauses to say what could happen
- to express supposition or probability in the past
- to refer to a future action expressed in the past.

(32) Translate: I would like to eat. I would prefer to eat now.
I would do it now.

9.10 Compound tenses: the perfect tense

Compound tenses have two parts – an auxiliary verb and a past participle. The two parts must never be separated.

The perfect tense is formed by using the present tense of *haber* (the auxiliary verb) plus the past participle of the verb you want to use.

haber	*comprar*	*comer*	*subir*		*cortarse*
he	*comprado*	*comido*	*subido*	*me he*	*cortado*
has				*te has*	
ha				*se ha*	
hemos				*nos hemos*	
habéis				*os habéis*	
han				*se han*	

Reflexive verbs in the perfect tense need the reflexive pronoun before the auxiliary verb *haber*.

¿Qué te ha pasado? Me he cortado el dedo.
(What's happened to you? I've cut my finger.)

Some common irregular past participles:
abrir → abierto; morir → muerto; cubrir → cubierto; poner → puesto; decir → dicho; romper → roto; escribir → escrito; ver → visto; hacer → hecho; volver → vuelto

Compound verbs have the same irregular past participle as the original verb.
descubrir → descubierto

 33 Use the verbs above to talk about what you have done recently.

The perfect tense is used in the same way as in English to indicate an action which began and ended in the same period of time as the speaker or writer is describing. It is used in a question which does not refer to any particular time.

▶ Two important exceptions:
  • to talk about how long something has been happening Spanish uses the present tense where English uses the perfect:
  Hace más de un mes que vivo aquí.
  (I have lived here for over a month.)

  • to translate 'to have just':
  acabar de – acabo de llegar (I have just arrived)

  • The perfect infinitive is formed by using the infinitive of the verb *haber* plus the appropriate past participle:
  De haberlo sabido ... (Having known this ...)

Translate: They have just finished eating. They have been eating for over an hour.

9.11 Compound tenses: the pluperfect tense

This is formed by using the imperfect of the auxiliary *haber* and the past participle of the verb required:
había, habías, había etc. + *comprado, comido, subido, dicho, hecho* etc.
Just as in English it is used to refer to an action which happened before another action took place in the past.
La cena ya se había terminado cuando ellos llegaron.
(The dinner had already finished when they arrived.)

▶ The same two exceptions apply as for the perfect tense:

• hacer in time clauses: where English uses the pluperfect 'had', Spanish uses the imperfect *hacía*.

• *acabar de* (to have just):
Acababa de llegar cuando empezó a llover.
(He had just arrived when it started to rain.)

9.12 The future and conditional perfects

Use the future or conditional of the auxiliary verb *haber* and the past participle of the verb required:
Habré terminado dentro de dos horas.
(I will have finished within two hours.)
Habría terminado antes pero no vi la hora.
(I would have finished sooner but I didn't see the time.)

(35) Translate: He had just eaten. They had been waiting for two days. I will have eaten by nine o clock. I could have eaten sooner.

9.13 Direct and indirect speech

▶ Direct speech is used when you quote the exact words spoken.

▶ Indirect speech is used when you want to explain or report what somebody said.

Remember you will need to change all parts of the sentence that relate to the speaker, not just the verb.

10 Verbs: The subjunctive mood

So far all the tenses explained have been in the indicative 'mood'.
Remember the subjunctive is not a tense but a verbal mood. For its uses
see 10.4. It is used a lot more in Spanish than it is in English.

10.1 The present subjunctive

This is formed by adding the following endings to the stem of the verb:
-ar: -e, -es, -e, -emos, -éis, -en
-er / -ir: -a, -as, -a, -amos, -áis, -an
Remember that some verbs need to change their spelling to preserve
their sound:
coger – coja, cojas etc. (*j* required before *a* or *o*)
pagar – pague, pagues etc. (*u* required after *g* before *e*)
cruzar – cruce, cruces etc. (*z* required only before *a* or *o*)

Remember that radical-changing verbs change their root vowel when
stressed; this applies equally in the present subjunctive:
dormir – duerma, duermas etc. (But note also: *durmimos, durmáis*)
jugar – juegue, juegues etc.
empezar – empiece, empieces etc.
pedir – pida, pidas etc. (But note also: *pidamos, pidáis*)

Irregular verbs
Many of these are not so irregular if you remember that they are formed
by taking the first person singular of the present indicative:
hacer → hago → haga, hagas, haga, hagamos, hagáis, hagan
Tener, caer, decir, oír, poner, salir, traer, venir and *ver* follow this pattern.
A few have an irregular stem: *dar → dé, des, dé, demos, deis, den*

 Write out the irregular subjunctive forms in full for:
estar – esté; haber – haya; ir – vaya; saber – sepa; ser – sea

10.2 The imperfect subjunctive

There are two forms of the imperfect subjunctive. Both are used but the
-ra form is slightly more common and is sometimes used as an
alternative to the conditional.

Take the third person plural of the preterite form minus the *-ron* ending
and add the following endings:

compra -ron	*comie -ron*	*subie -ron*
comprara/se	*comiera/se*	*subiera/se*
compraras/ses	*comieras/ses*	*subieras/ses*
comprara/se	*comiera/se*	*subiera/se*
compráramos/semos	*comiéramos/semos*	*subiéramos/semos*
comprarais/seis	*comierais/seis*	*subierais/seis*
compraran/sen	*comieran/sen*	*subieran/sen*

Spelling change, radical-changing and irregular verbs all follow this rule too.

hacer → *hicieron* → *hiciera, hicieras*   *pedir* → *pidieron* → *pidiera, pidieras*
tener → *tuvieron* → *tuviera, tuvieras*   *dormir* → *durmieron* → *durmiera,*
                                                                                        durmieras
                                                           oír → *oyeron* → *oyera, oyeras*

10.3 The perfect and pluperfect subjunctives

These both use the auxiliary verb *haber* plus the past participle.

The perfect uses the present subjunctive:	The pluperfect uses the imperfect subjunctive:
haya comprado	*hubiera / hubiese comido*
hayas comprado	*hubieras / hubieses comido*
haya comprado	*hubiera / hubiese comido*
hayamos comprado	*hubiéramos / hubiésemos comido*
hayáis comprado	*hubierais / hubieseis comido*
hayan comprado	*hubieran / hubiesen comido*

10.4 Uses of the subjunctive

The subjunctive is used widely in Spanish.

▶ When there are two different clauses in the sentence and the subject of one verb

  • influences the other (advising, requesting, ordering)

  • expresses a preference, like or dislike (with *gustar, odiar, alegrarse*)

  • expresses feelings of fear, regret, doubt or possibility

▶ With impersonal expressions with adjectives

▶ After expressions of purpose

▶ After expressions referring to a future action

▶ After expressions referring to concessions or conditions – 'provided that', 'unless'

▶ In clauses describing a non-existent or indefinite noun

▶ In main clauses; after *ojalá* (if only); after words indicating 'perhaps' (*tal vez, quizás*); after *como si* (as if); after *aunque* meaning 'even if' (but not 'although')

▶ In set phrases:
  digan lo que digan (whatever they say), *sea lo que sea* (be that as it may), *pase lo que pase* (whatever happens)

▶ After words ending in *-quiera* ('-ever')
  cualquiera (whatever), *dondequiera* (wherever)

Grammar Summary

Don't forget that when you make a sentence negative this often gives it an element of doubt:
Creo que llegarán a tiempo. (I think they will arrive in time.)
but
No creo que lleguen a tiempo. (I don't think they will arrive in time.)
Note the sequence of tenses using the subjunctive:

main verb	subjunctive verb
present / future / future perfect / imperative	present or perfect
any other tense (including conditional)	imperfect or pluperfect

Exceptions:
'If I were to do what you are saying' = imperfect subjunctive:
Si hiciera lo que me dices
'If I had' + past participle = pluperfect subjunctive:
Si lo hubiera sabido:
(If [only] I had known)

(37) Write sentences to illustrate each of the usages listed above and use all tenses of the subjunctive.

11 The imperative

The imperative is used for giving commands and instructions.
Positive form:

	tú	*vosotros/as*	*usted*	*ustedes*
comprar	*compra*	*comprad*	*compre*	*compren*
comer	*come*	*comed*	*coma*	*coman*
subir	*sube*	*subid*	*suba*	*suban*

Irregular verbs in the tú form:
decir → di, hacer → haz, oír → oye, poner → pon, salir → sal, saber → sé, tener → ten, venir → ven, ver → ve
NB Reflexive forms in the *vosotros* form drop the final *d* before adding -*os*:
levantad + os = levantaos, sentad + os = sentaos
and the final *s* in the *nosotros* form before adding -*nos*:
levantemos + nos = levantémonos, sentemos + nos = sentémonos.
(Notice that you need to add a written accent because the stressed syllable is now two from the end of the word.)
Exception: *irse → idos*
All negative forms are the same as the present subjunctive.
Note that the positive and negative forms for *usted* and *ustedes* are the same.
Remember the use of the infinitive to give impersonal negative commands:
No fumar (No smoking)

(38) Give orders in all forms using the following verbs:
salir, acostarse, dormir, cantar, correr.

12 Reflexive verbs

The reflexive pronoun – *me, te, se, nos, os, se* – is attached to the end of the infinitive form, the gerund and the positive imperative, but is placed before all other forms.

▶ True reflexive forms are actions done to oneself:
Me lavé la cara. (I washed my face.)
but
Lavé el coche de mi tío. (I washed my uncle's car.)

▶ Some verbs change their meaning slightly in the reflexive form:
dormir (to sleep) – *dormirse* (to fall asleep)
poner (to carry) – *ponerse* (to put on [clothes])

▶ Use the reflexive pronoun to mean 'each other':
Nos miramos el uno al otro. (We looked at one another.)

▶ The reflexive form is often used to avoid the passive (see section 13).

(39) **Translate: They got up early. I showered and dressed. We put on our school uniform.**

13 The passive

The passive is used less in Spanish than in English and mostly in written form only. The structure is similar to English.
Use the appropriate form of ser plus the past participle which **must agree** with the noun, and use por if you need to add by whom the action is taken.
La iglesia ha sido convertida en un museo.
(The church has been converted into a museum.)
La ventana fue rota por los chicos que jugaban en la calle.
(The window was broken by the children who were playing in the street.)
There are several ways to avoid using the passive in Spanish:

▶ Rearrange the sentence into an active format but remember to use a direct object pronoun.

▶ Use the reflexive pronoun *se*.

▶ Use the third person plural with an active verb.

(40) **Translate: The cup was broken by the waiter. The cake was served to me on a plate.**

14 Ser and estar

Both these verbs mean 'to be' but they are used in different circumstances.

▶ *Ser* denotes time and a permanent situation or quality, character or origin.

▶ It is also used in impersonal expressions and with the past participle to form the passive.

▶ *Estar* denotes position, temporary situation, state of health or mood.

▶ It indicates when a change has taken place.
¿Está vivo o está muerto? Está muerto.
(Is he alive or dead [now]? He is dead.)
Mi hermano estaba casado pero ya está divorciado.
(My brother used to be married but now he's divorced.)

(41) **Write sentences to illustrate each of the points made above.**

▶ Some adjectives have a different nuance depending on whether they are used with *ser* or *estar*:

Mi hermana es bonita. (My sister is pretty.)
Mi hermana está bonita hoy. (My sister is looking pretty today.)
while other adjectives change their meaning depending on whether they are used with *ser* or *estar*: *listo, aburrido, bueno, cansado, malo, nuevo, vivo, triste*

(42) **Translate the list above, giving both meanings for each adjective.**

15 Some verbs frequently used in the third person

The subject is often a singular or plural idea, activity or thing, rather than a person.
gustar, encantar, interesar, molestar, preocupar, hacer falta

16 Impersonal verbs

se is often used to indicate the idea of 'one', 'you' or 'we' in a general way (often in notices) and to avoid the passive in Spanish:
Aquí se habla inglés (English spoken here)
Se prohíbe tirar basura (Do not throw litter)
No se puede entrar (No entry)
Another useful impersonal expression is *hay que*:
Hay que salir por aquí. (You have to go out this way.)
Other impersonal verbs are *llover* (to rain) and *nevar (to snow)* and expressions of weather with *hacer*.
Sections 17–22 can be found in the Students' Book.

infinitive	present	preterite	imperfect	future	conditional	present subjunctive	imperfect subjunctive	present participle	past participle
comprar	compro	compré	compraba	compraré	compraría	compre	comprara/se	comprando	comprado
to buy	I buy	I bought	I used to buy	I will buy	I would buy	buy	bought	buying	bought
comer	como	comí	comía	comeré	comería	coma	comiera/se	comiendo	comido
subir	subo	subí	subía	subiré	subiría	suba	subiera/se	subiendo	subido
levantarse	me levanto	me levanté	me levantaba	me levantaré	me levantaría	me levante	me levantara/se	levantádome	levantado
dar	doy	di	daba	daré	daría	dé	diera/se	dando	dado
decir	digo	dije	decía	diré	diría	diga	dijera/se	diciendo	dicho
estar	estoy	estuve	estaba	estaré	estaría	esté	estuviera/se	estando	estado
haber	he	hube	había	habré	habría	haya	hubiera/se	habiendo	habido
hacer	hago	hice	hacía	haré	haría	haga	hiciera/se	haciendo	hecho
ir	voy	fui	iba	iré	iría	vaya	fuera/se	yendo	ido
poder	puedo	pude	podía	podré	podría	pueda	pudiera/se	pudiendo	podido
poner	pongo	puse	ponía	pondré	pondría	ponga	pusiera/se	poniendo	puesto
querer	quiero	quise	quería	querré	querría	quiera	quisiera/se	queriendo	querido
saber	sé	supe	sabía	sabré	sabría	sepa	supiera/se	sabiendo	sabido
ser	soy	fui	era	seré	sería	sea	fuera/se	siendo	sido
tener	tengo	tuve	tenía	tendré	tendría	tenga	tuviera/se	teniendo	tenido
traer	traigo	traje	traía	traeré	traería	traiga	trajera/se	trayendo	traído
venir	vengo	vine	venía	vendré	vendría	venga	viniera/se	viniendo	venido

Pronunciation

When you are speaking Spanish try to imagine yourself as a Spanish person.

Read aloud to get used to the sound of your own voice in Spanish.

Practise the sounds in front of a mirror – it helps if you can see the way your mouth moves to produce the different sounds.

Record a simple song or an advert and imitate it.

Practise asking questions then answering them yourself.

Beware of reverting to an English accent when you see a word in Spanish which looks like an English word: *televisión* / television.

Make sure you know how to say the alphabet in Spanish in order to spell out words.

The Spanish alphabet: listen to the sounds and repeat them. (Track 6)
A B C D E F G ... H I J K L M ... N Ñ O P Q R ... S T U V W ... X Y Z
It helps to learn them in groups. Sing them to one of your favourite tunes.
Note: *Ññ* is a separate letter in Spanish and comes after *N* in alphabetical lists. All the letters are feminine.

The vowel sounds
Spanish vowels are always clearly pronounced and not relaxed in unstressed syllables as happens in English. **Listen and practise the vowels. (Track 7)**
Alba Arbalaez abre su abanico amarillo amablemente.
Enrique Esquivel escoge el edredón más elegante.
Inés Iglesias indica que es imposible ingresar allí.
Óscar Ordóñez odia las hojas otoñales.
Umberto Umbral usa un uniforme ultramoderno.

Consonants
Spanish *g* is pronounced hard as in 'gate' before *a, o* or *u* and soft like an exaggerated English 'h' before *e* and *i*.
Spanish *c* is pronounced hard as in 'cow' before *a, o* or *u* and soft as in 'thing' before *e* and *i*.

3 Practise these sounds. (Track 8)

hard *c*: *caballo, conejo, culebra*	**hard** *g* : *gato, gorila, gusano*
soft *c* : *cero, cisne*	**soft** *g* : *gente, gimnasta*

Some spellings change to preserve the sounds:
The hard *c* sound as in 'cow' is written *qu* before *e* or *i*: *sacar* but *saqué*
The hard *g* sound as in 'gate' is written *gu* before *e* or *i*: *pagar* but *pagué*
The soft *c* sound as in 'thing' is written *z* before *a* or *o*: *empecé* but *empezar*
The soft *g* sound like an exaggerated English 'h' is written *j* before *a* or *o*: *coger* but *cojo*
The sound *gu* as in 'guava' is written *gü* before e or i: *averiguar* but *averigüé*

The position of a consonant in the word also affects its sound: a consonant at the beginning of a word is usually pronounced harder than in the middle or at the end.

La letra d: (Track 9)		**La letra r:**
donde	*adonde*	*revista pero*
dámelo	*me lo ha dado*	**La letra s:**
drogas	*cuidado*	*sí me gustan las tapas*
La letra ll:		*suelen ser muy malas*
llegar	*Sevilla*	**La letra x:**
		exacto taxi, texto

Try to read out the following tongue-twisters. Compare your pronunciation with the recording. (Track 10)

Es verdad que la ventana verde está en Madrid.
Llora la llama cuando llueve. Que no llore la llama cuando llueva.

Jorge juega ajedrez. Jugando ajedrez Jorge juró jugar con justicia.
Listen to the difference between the words *pero* and *perro*. If you have problems with this sound in Spanish, listen and practise it as much as you can. (Track 11)

The letter *r* sounds softer in the middle of a word – *pero, Pedro* – and harder at the beginning of a word: *revista, Roberto*

Double *rr* sounds strongest:
Llora la guitarra con rabia y dulzura.
El perro comió una pera. Pero la perra no comió el peral.

Once you have mastered all the different sounds you need to make sure you are confident about where to place the stress on each word.

Here is the basic rule:

In words which end in a vowel, *s* or *n* the spoken stress falls naturally on the second to last syllable: *instrumento, importantes, representan.*

In words which end in a consonant (except *s* or *n*) the stress falls naturally on the last syllable: *animal, alrededor, nariz.*

All words which do **not** follow this rule require a written accent to indicate where the spoken stress falls: *última, histórico, tecnología.*

Spoken stress and vowels

For the purposes of stress *a, e* and *o* are considered to be 'strong' vowels, and *i* and *u* are considered 'weak'.

▶ If the spoken stress falls on a syllable containing two vowels then the stronger one is stressed: *oficial* (pronounced *oficial not oficial*).

▶ If both are strong vowels, they are considered to be separate syllables: *levantaos* (pronounced *levantaos*).

▶ If both are weak vowels then the stress falls on the second one: *cuida* (pronounced *cuida* not *cuida*).

▶ If the word does **not** follow these rules then the stress is marked by a written accent: *país, queríamos.*

Finally, having practised all these individual sounds, you need to make sure the whole sentence sounds Spanish.

Intonation (Track 12)

Your voice should rise and fall when you speak.

In Spanish it should fall:

▶ at the end of a short sentence. *Toco la guitarra.* (I play the guitar.)

▶ at the end of a question with an interrogative: *¿Qué instrumento tocas?* (What instrument do you play?)

It should rise:

▶ at the end of another type of question: *¿Tienes una flauta?* (Have you got a flute?)

▶ in the middle of longer sentences:
Tú tienes una flauta y yo tengo una guitarra.
(You've got a flute and I've got a guitar.)

Sound linking (Track 13)

In spoken Spanish, vowel sounds and consonants slide into each other, which helps to make the sentence flow.

When vowel sounds end and begin consecutive words they are linked together. This is known as *sinalefa*.

A final consonant is linked together with a following vowel. This is known as *entrelazamiento*.

1 Copy these words and phrases and indicate the *sinalefa* and *entrelazamiento*.

El otoño: isla
de perfil estricto
que pone en olvido
la onda indecisa.

¡Amor a la línea!
La vid se desnuda
de una vestidura
demasiado rica

2 Listen to these verses and try to imitate the pronunciation.

¡Oh claridad! Pía
tanto entre las hojas
que quieren ser todas
a un tiempo amarillas.

¡Trabazón de brisas
entre cielo y álamo!
Y todo el espacio,
tan continuo, vibra

Esta luz antigua
de tarde feliz
no puede morir.
¡Ya es mía, ya es mía!

It's always a good idea to **do something** with the words you are trying to learn, rather than just looking at them. Here are some ideas to try.

▶ Group the words you are learning, for example by writing lists of synonyms (similar words) or antonyms (opposites):

la victoria / la derrota (victory / defeat); ganar / perder (to win / to lose); activo / perezoso (active / lazy)

▶ List words in 'families'. If you have noted the verb, can you find a noun or an adjective which is related to it?

comprender (to understand) la comprensión   comprensivo/a
exigir (to demand)   la exigencia   exigente
mentir (to lie)   la mentira   mentiroso/a

▶ Write out a set of words in jumbled form, then come back a few days later and try to unjumble them.

▶ Can you sort out these eight words on the topic of smoking and drinking?

1) mrufa, 2) qstbaioamu, 3) lloohac, 4) rabrorecha, 5) onicov, 6) ploocpa, 7) lomunpes, 8) dihorobip

6) alcopop, 7) pulmones, 8) prohibido

1) fumar, 2) tabaquismo, 3) alcohol, 4) borrachera, 5) nocivo,

▶ Write out words with gaps for missing letters or sentences with key words gapped and then try to fill them in later.

▶ Complete these words which are all linked to newspapers:

1) dia-io, 2) -en-ual, 3) pu-lici-ad, 4) c-ti-iano, 5) le-to-, 6) re-orta-e

6) reportaje

1) diario, 2) mensual, 3) publicidad, 4) cotidiano, 5) lector,

▶ Choose, say, three words from a particular topic area and challenge yourself to say or write a sentence including them all. Try the following:

el divorcio – la pareja – monopariente
equilibrado – peso – la forma
el empleo – el paro – la remuneración

▶ Make a wordsearch using as many words from one topic as you can, then solve it a week later when you have forgotten where you put them.

Frases clave

no sólo ... sino también	*not only ... but also*
tanto ... como / tan ... como	*as much as*
me gustaría	*I would like*
me molesta	*it annoys me*
me fascina	*it fascinates me*
paso horas ... -ando/-iendo	*I spend hours ... -ing*
¿Cuánto tiempo hace / hacía que ... ?	*How long have / had you ...*
¿Desde cuándo?	*Since when?*
tengo ganas de + *infinitive*	*I fancy ... -ing / want to*
no me da la gana + *infinitive*	*I don't want to*
prefiero que + *subjunctive*	*I prefer that*
insisto que	*I insist that*
nos aconseja que	*he / she advises us to*
volver a hacer	*to do again*
ponerse a hacer	*to set about doing / to begin*
acabo de llegar	*I have just arrived*
acababa de llegar	*I had just arrived*
hace una hora	*an hour ago*
nos hace falta	*we need / lack*
llevo cinco años ... -ando/-iendo	*I have been ... -ing for five years*
es escandaloso que + *subjunctive*	*it's scandalous that*
es decepcionante que + *subjunctive*	*it's disappointing that*
es una lástima que + *subjunctive*	*it's a shame that*
me alegra que + *subjunctive*	*I'm happy that*
me preocupa que + *subjunctive*	*I'm worried that*
¡Qué bien que + *subjunctive*	*It's good that*
me parece muy bien que + *subjunctive*	*I think it's great that*
no me sorprende que	*it doesn't surprise me that*
tratar de hacer algo	*to try to do something*
trata de	*it's about*
creo que	*I believe that*
se supone que	*it is supposed that*
no se puede negar	*it can't be denied that*
hay que considerar que	*you have to consider that*
por un lado ... por el otro	*on the one hand ... on the other*
lo bueno / malo es que	*the good / bad thing is that*
lo mejor / peor es que	*the best / worst thing is that*
lo que (no) me gusta	*what I (don't) like*
no se permite	*it's not allowed*
sin embargo	*nevertheless / however*

al mismo tiempo	*at the same time*
además	*besides*
claro que sí	*of course*
a la edad de	*at the age of*
en cambio	*on the other hand*
no tiene nada que ver con	*it's got nothing to do with*
tengo la intención de	*I intend to*
quisiera	*I would like*
me hubiera gustado	*I would have liked*
yo que tú + *conditional*	*if I were you + conditional*
basta ya	*that's enough*
por la calle	*down the road*
a fin de cuentas	*after all / when all's said and done*
en cuanto a	*as for*
estoy de acuerdo contigo	*I agree with you*
soler + *infinitive*	*to be in the habit of doing something*
(used in present and imperfect only)	
se me hace que	*I think / I've a feeling that*
sin lugar a dudas	*without a doubt*
digan lo que digan	*they can say what they like*
pase lo que pase	*whatever happens*
sea como sea	*however / whatever*
a mi modo de ver	*as far as I'm concerned*
a mi parecer	*in my opinion*
en primer lugar	*in the first place*
en cuanto a	*as for*
sería mejor + *infinitive*	*it would be better to*
Three verbs meaning to 'become'	
hacerse; llegar a ser; convertirse en	

Puente – Frases clave

¡Qué listo eres!	*How clever you are!*
¿Está listo?	*Are you ready?*
las comunidades autónomas (CCAA)	*the self-governing regions*
unas cincuenta personas	*about fifty people*
a lo alto de	*to the top of*
suelo visitar	*I usually visit*
ni el uno ni el otro	*neither one nor the other*
a orillas del mar	*at the sea side*
no solo … sino también	*not only … but also*
sin duda alguna	*without a doubt*

Vocabulary

Puente – Topics vocabulary

mejor / peor	*better / worse*
mayor / menor	*greater, older / lesser, younger*
actual	*present day, current*
vasco	*basque*
sin igual	*unequalled*
animada	*lively*
una obra maestra	*a work of art*
el paisaje	*countryside*
atroz	*atrocious*
extraño	*strange*
pintoresco	*picturesque*
por supuesto	*of course*
ecologico / la ecología	*ecological / ecology*
la selva	*jungle*
el cincuenta por ciento	*fifty per cent*
kilómetros cuadrados	*square kilometres*
la superficie	*surface area*
gozar de	*to enjoy*
indígena	*native / indigenous*
en el extranjero	*abroad*
actor / actriz	*actor / actress*
ambos	*both*
orgulloso	*proud*
la vega	*orchard / cultivated land*
el espejo	*mirror*
fregar los platos	*to wash the dishes*

Unit 1 – Frases clave

me parece a mí	*it seems to me*
vale, de acuerdo	*OK, I agree*
en cambio	*on the other hand*
no comparto tu opinión	*I don't share your opinion*
cinco sobre diez	*five out of ten*
me molesta / preocupa	*it bothers me / worries me*
es mi opinión considerada	*it is my considered opinion*
dar en el clavo	*to hit the nail on the head*
al cien por cien	*one hundred per cent*

Unit 1 – Topic vocabulary

los concursos	*quiz shows*
las tertulias	*chat shows*
las retransmisiones deportivas	*sports reports*
el telediario	*daily news programme*
los dibujos animados	*cartoons*
la pantalla	*screen*
tampoco	*neither*
la tercera / cuarta parte	*a third / half*
la mitad	*a half*
la mayoría	*the majority*
intruso	*intrusive*
inocuo	*harmless*
morboso	*morbid*
humillante	*humiliating*
una broma	*a joke*
asimismo	*likewise*
la telebasura	*junk television*
no obstante	*nevertheless*
exigir	*to demand / insist upon*
la meta	*the aim*
el cotilleo	*chitchat / rumour*
semanal / quincenal / mensual	*weekly / fortnightly / monthly*
a diario / cotidiano	*daily*
divertido	*amusing*
frívolo	*frivolous / silly*
salaz	*salacious / saucy*

Unit 2 – Frases clave

se conecta	*it is connected*
se emiten señales	*it sends out signals*
sino que	*but / except / rather*
es algo efímero	*it's something temporary*
carece de	*it lacks / doesn't have*
no se permite	*it isn't allowed*
ponerse en contacto con	*to get in touch with*
no me importa (que)	*it doesn't bother me (that)*
me sorprende que + *subjunctive*	*it surprises me that*
navegar por Internet	*to surf the Net*

Unit 2 – Topic vocabulary

la energía solar	*solar power*
portátil	*portable*
un aparato	*a piece of equipment*
un mando a distancia	*a remote control*
enchufarse	*to plug in*
un auricular	*an earpiece*
a la vez	*at the same time*
descargar	*to download*
los ficheros	*tracks (music) / files*
comprobar	*to prove*
un internauta	*internet user / surfer*
merecer	*to merit / deserve*
la pantalla táctil	*touch screen*
los altavoces	*loudspeakers*
un lector MP3	*an MP3 reader*
un bloguero	*a blogger*
incidir en	*to have an influence / a bearing on*
el correo electrónico	*email*
apoderarse de	*to take charge of*
el crecimiento	*growth / rise*
el aislamiento	*isolation*
la piratería	*piracy*
amenazada	*threatened*
el lavado de cerebro	*brainwashing*
en cualquier lugar	*anywhere*
aprovecharse de	*to take advantage of*

Unit 3 – Frases clave

lo que más me gusta	*what I like most*
lo mejor / peor	*the best / worst thing*
de tal palo tal astilla	*chip off the old block / like father like son*
hay que considerar	*you must think about*
no se puede negar	*you can't deny*

Unit 3 – Topic vocabulary

el protagonista	*main character / protagonist*
el guionista / el guión	*scriptwriter / script*
desempeñar un papel	*to play a role*

rodar una película / el rodaje	*to shoot a film / film shoot*
el estreno / estrenar	*premier / to premier*
la pantalla	*screen*
chocante	*shocking*
distraer	*to distract*
desarrollarse	*to develop / take place*
un goya	*Spanish equivalent to Oscar*
la gemela	*twin sister*
tener éxito	*to be a success*
el enfoque / enfocarse en	*the focus / to focus on*
un premio	*a prize*
una beca	*a scholarship*
un largo / corto metraje	*full-length film / short*
destacarse	*to stand out*
el pueblo español	*the Spanish people*
un títere	*a puppet*
una máscara	*a mask*
un espectáculo	*a show / spectacle*
la cárcel	*prison*
encarcelado	*imprisoned*
una condena	*a sentence (prison)*
un delito	*a crime*
un preso / una presa	*male / female prisoner*
un cantautor / una cantautora	*singer-songwriter*
tocar un instrumento	*to play an instrument*
ciego	*blind*
la penuria	*abject poverty*

Unit 4 – Frases clave

de promedio	*on average*
lo que les de la gana	*whatever pleases them*
ni siquiera	*not even*
estar dispuesto a	*to be prepared to (do something)*
tener en cuenta	*to bear in mind / be mindful of*
¡Ojalá (que)	*If only / I wish (that)*
Don Nadie	*Mister Nobody*
cabe mencionar	*it's worth mentioning*
se remonta a	*it goes back to / it owes itself to*
sin ánimo de lucro	*unrewarded / charitable*
comparecer ante un tribunal	*to come before a magistrate*

Unit 4 – Topic vocabulary

los prejuicios	*prejudices*
compartir	*to share*
la etnía	*ethnicity*
xenófobo	*xenophobe*
pijo	*fashionable*
inculcar	*to indoctrinate*
la desgana	*lethargy / lack of enthusiasm*
holgazán / holgazanear	*lazy / to be lazy*
luchar (por)	*to struggle / fight (for)*
antaño	*yesteryear / long ago*
asequible / inasequible	*attainable / unattainable*
emprendedor	*enterprising / go-ahead*
lograr	*to succeed / gain*
consigo mismo	*with(in) oneself*
el amor propio	*self-worth / esteem*
discrepar	*to differ in opinion*
a pesar de	*in spite of*
las cuadrillas	*gangs of youths*
el argot	*slang*
los honorarios	*fee*
el hurto pequeño	*small-time theft*
arraigado	*firmly rooted*

Unit 5 – Frases clave

se necesita	*you need*
¿Con qué se juega?	*What do you play it with?*
cada vez más (arriesgado)	*more and more (risky)*
serán las dos	*it'll be about two o'clock*
tengo la intención de + *infinitive*	*I intend to*
cuento con + *infinitive*	*I'm counting on*
quisiera + *infinitive*	*I would like to*
yo que tú + *conditional*	*If I were you + conditional*
sería mejor	*it would be better*

Unit 5 – Topic vocabulary

mantenerse en forma	*to keep fit*
la maña	*skill / trick*
recuperarse	*to get fit after an illness*
entrenarse (para un maratón)	*to train (for a marathon)*
el relajamiento / relajarse	*relaxation / to relax*

un buen estado de salud	*a good state of health*
los huesos / los pulmones	*bones / lungs*
los beneficios del deporte	*the benefits of sport*
respirar	*to breathe*
luchar contra el sobrepeso	*to battle against overweight*
quemar las calorías	*to burn off the calories*
la confianza en si mismo	*self-confidence*
una medalla de oro	*a gold medal*
la herida	*injury*
los campeonatos mundiales	*world championships*
ganar / perder / participar en	*to win / to lose / to take part in*
hacer trampa	*to cheat*
la victoria / la derrota	*victory / defeat*
el triunfo / triunfar	*triumph*
ganar el respeto de otros	*to be respected by others*
el adversario / compañero de equipo	*opponent / team-mate*
el árbitro / los oficiales	*the referee / the officials*
el dopaje	*drug-taking (in sport)*
el comportamiento	*behaviour*
rechazar la violencia / el racismo	*to reject violence / racism*

Unit 6 – Frases clave

bajo la influencia de	*under the influence of*
después de haber + *past participle*	*after having done something*
al haber bebido	*having drunk*
debería de haber + *past participle*	*he ought to have done something*
de haberlo sabido	*if only I had known*
estaba ignorando	*I wasn't taking any notice of*

Unit 6 – Topic vocabulary

parar	*to stop*
el pasajero	*passenger*
sensato	*sensible*
sensible	*sensitive*
el riesgo	*the risk*
el consumo de	*the consumption of*
el botellón	*binge drinking*
de hecho	*of course*
un drogadicto	*a drugadict*
drogarse	*to take drugs*
el tabaquismo	*smoking*

el fumador	*smoker*
prohibir	*to forbid*
incitar a	*to incite*
renunciar a	*to give up*
conformarse	*to conform*
el aceite de oliva	*olive oil*
escalofriante	*chilling / mind-blowing*
el equilibrio	*balance*
el alimento	*food*
la grasa	*fatty foods*
el capricho	*fad*
cuidarse	*to look after oneself*
el cuerpo	*the body*
la mente	*the mind*

Unit 7 – Frases clave

me apasiona	*I love*
me agrada	*it pleases me*
¡Cómo mola, tío!	*Wow!*
trasvasar el agua	*to pipe water from one place to another*
promover el turismo	*to promote tourism*
P.D. (post data)	*P.S. (post script)*
de bajo coste	*budget (airline) / low-cost*
se me hace que + *subjunctive*	*it seems to me that*
se teme que + *subjunctive*	*it's feared that*
el efecto invernadero	*greenhouse effect*

Unit 7 – Topic vocabulary

Pascua	*Easter*
indígena	*native / indigenous*
las cuevas	*caves*
una media	*average*
deslumbrar	*to dazzle*
el legado	*the legacy*
alojarse	*to stay in a hotel*
cotidiana	*daily*
alucinantes	*spectacular*
ideóneo	*ideal*
el medio ambiente	*the environment*
la basura	*rubbish*

el sendero	*pathway*
apagar	*to put out (cigarette)*
las cancelas	*gates*
el ganado	*cattle*
la veda	*prohibition*
cumplir con	*to comply / do as asked*
las instalaciones	*facilities*
ingresos	*income*
el retraso	*the delay*
aguardar	*to await (reply)*
aterrizar	*to land (aircraft)*
fracasar	*to fail*
nocivo	*harmful*

Unit 8 – Frases claves

¡Caramba!	*Good heavens!*
¡Qué pena!	*What a shame!*
llevarse bien / mal con	*to get on well / badly with*
algunos dirían que	*some people might say*
podrías pensar que	*you might think that*
es imprescindible que + *subjunctive*	*it is essential that*
salir del armario	*to come out (figurative)*
hacer daño	*to harm*
hacer quiebra / quebrar	*to go bust / bankrupt*
ahorrar dinero	*to save money*

Unit 8 – Topic vocabulary

regañar	*to scold / tell off*
entenderse con	*to get on (well) with*
discutir	*to argue*
confiar en	*to confide in*
confiarse de	*to have confidence in*
callarse	*to keep quiet*
escandalizarse	*to make a fuss*
las normas	*rules and regulations / code of conduct*
comprensivo	*understanding*
los derechos	*rights*
los bisabuelos	*great grandparents*
las expectativas	*expectations*
el ombligo	*tummy button*
la pandilla	*the group / crowd*

emborracharse	*to get drunk*
rebelarse	*to rebel*
riesgo / arriesgarse	*risk / to take a risk*
según	*according to*
estar casado / divorciado	*to be married / divorced*
una pareja	*a pair / partner*
pelearse	*to fight / have a fight*
atropellar	*to knock down / run over*
convivir	*to live together*

Unit 9 – Frases clave

ser fuerte en	*to be good at (subject)*
aprobar los examenes	*to pass exams*
suspender un examen	*to fail an exam*
llevar a cabo	*to carry out / to take place*
hacer payasadas	*act the fool / play the clown*
cara o cruz	*heads or tails*
la tasa de desempleo	*rate / level of unemployment*
es de suma importancia	*it is of the greatest importance*
concertar una cita	*to agree a meeting date / book an appointment*

Unit 9 – Topic vocabulary

fugarse	*to skip lessons (escape from school)*
la formación	*training*
fontanero	*plumber*
albañil	*brick-layer*
obrero	*worker*
maestro/a	*schoolteacher*
la docencia	*schooling*
novedoso	*innovative*
abarcar	*to take on / cover*
aprendizaje	*learning*
encabezar	*to head up / lead*
ventaja / desventaja	*advantage / disadvantage*
surgir	*to appear*
autoestima	*self-esteem*
consejos / aconsejar	*advice / to advise*
agobiante	*overwhelming*
repasar	*to revise*
revalidar	*to retake an exam*
fallar	*to fail / not work*

Listening task 1

1) children over 16 only allowed;
owner had spent a fortune on restoration;
dishes served not suitable for young children
2) negative / surprised – Spain is usually more tolerant of children;
question legality; law to protect children's rights?
3) Families need to state ages of children when booking;
insists most customers agree with the decision and even
welcome it – they dislike eating surrounded by noisy children

Listening task 2

1) T; 2) N; 3) T; 4) N; 5) T; 6) P

Paraphrasing underlined text:
1) no es justo
2) no me importa
3) que sí valen la pena
4) niña
5) haber ... precauciones con la propaganda dirigida a los peques
6) nos encanta

Listening task 3

1) en patines;   2) 27 provincias;   3) diariamente;
4) terrenos;   5) cien días;   6) una caravana

Listening task 4

1) c; 2) b; 3) a; 4) c; 5) b

Reading task 1

1) F; 2) V; 3) F; 4) V; 5) N;
6) V; 7) F; 8) N; 9) F; 10) N

Reading task 2

1) Trata de la Guerra Civil de España.
2) Las víctimas y el dictador y los generales de la Guerra Civil.
3) El Parlamento reconoció la existencia de las víctimas por primera vez.
4) Dieron permiso a las Comunidades Autónomas para buscar los
cadáveres de las víctimas sepultadas.
5) Significa que todos acordaron no hablar de la Guerra Civil; trataron de
olvidarse de los eventos del pasado.

Reading task 3

1) bonita;   2) mucho;   3) permitir;   4) quieren;
5) importante; 6) apariencia; 7) cierto;   8) de

Reading task 4

a) 3; b) 7; c) 1; d) 8; e) 9;
f) 11; g) 2; h) 6; i) 5; j) 10
(4 is the spare answer)

Note: where students are asked to write their own lists or examples these can be checked against the relevant section in the Students' Book.

1) Masculine: rivers, seas, lakes, mountains, cars, colours, weekdays, compass; Feminine: islands, roads, letter, most countries, cities and towns

2) *el / la policía* (policeman / police force); *el / la guía* (guide or leader / guidebook); *el / la orden* (arrangement or sequence / command); *el / la pendiente* (earring / slope)

3) *los reyes; los pades/ los deberes; los lápices; los martes*

4) When referring to nationality, profession, religion or status

5) this (near speaker), that (near person spoken to), that (over there)

6) *Voy a lavarme el pelo. Tu camiseta es más bonita que la mía. El bocadillo de jamón es tuyo y el mío es de queso. Su casa (de ellos) es más grande que la nuestra.*

8) *antiguo; diferente; varios; nuevo; medio; mismo; puro*

12) *por la calle; por avión; es para ti; por qué; para qué*

13) *Tengo un hermano menor y quiero a mi hermana mayor.*

14) When the word that follows begins with *i* or *hi* / *o* or *ho*

16) *tú / vosotros* = 'you' informal singular / plural/ *usted / ustedes* = 'you' formal singular / plural

18) *Quiero darle un libro. No, Pepe quiere dárselo.*

19) *Tiene que levantarse temprano mañana. Vete / Váyase / Idos / Váyanse. Estoy mirándola. Dáselo ahora.*

21) *Ese es el traje que me gusta; Jim es un estudiante conquien trabajo.*

22) Start with an inverted question mark / exclamation mark.

30) *Acababa de llegar cuando empezó a llover. Llovió durante todo el día y cuando estaba corriendo a casa de repente cesó de llover y salió el sol.*

32) *Me gustaría comer. Preferiría comer ahora. Lo haría ahora.*

34) *Acaban de comer. Hace más de una hora que comen* (or: *Han estado comiendo por más de una hora*).

35) *Acababa de comer. Hacía dos días que esperaban. Habré comid antes de las nueve. He podido comer más temprano.*

38) *sal / salga / salid / salgan; acuéstate / acuéstese / acostaos / acuéstense; duerme / duerma / dormid / duerman; canta /cante / cantad / canten; corre / corra / corred / corran*

39) *Se levantaron temprano. Me duché y me vestí. Nos pusimos el uniforme.*

42) *La taza fue rota por el mesero. Me sirvieron el pudín en un plato.*